HOW TO THINK LIKE A BOSS
And Get Ahead At Work

HOW TO THINK

LIKE A BOSS

And Get Ahead At Work

Barry Eigen

A Lyle Stuart Book
Published by Carol Publishing Group

A Lyle Stuart Book
Published by Carol Publishing Group

Editorial Offices
600 Madison Avenue
New York, NY 10022

Sales & Distribution Offices
120 Enterprise Avenue
Secaucus, NJ 07094

In Canada: Musson Book Company
A division of General Publishing Co. Limited
Don Mills, Ontario

Manufactured in the United States of America

Library of Congress Cataloging-in-Publication Data

Eigen, Barry.
    How to think like a boss : and get ahead at work / Barry Eigen.
      p. cm.
    "A Lyle Stuart book."
    ISBN 0-8184-0537-6 : $18.95
      1. Supervision of employees.   2. Personnel management.
    3. Executive ability.   I. Title.
    HF5549.12.E34   1990
    658.4'09—dc20   90-2195
                                                                  CIP

Carol Publishing Group books are available at special discounts for
bulk purchases, for sales promotions, premiums, fund raising, or
educational use. Special editions can also be created to specifica-
tions. For details contact: Special Sales Department, Carol Publishing Group, 120 Enterprise Avenue, Secaucus, NJ 07094

To the memory of my father,
DAVID F. EIGEN

Acknowledgments

To William Kesselman, the community pharmacist with whom I founded HealthCall Corporation (originally Sickroom Service, Inc.) and whose drug store served as its launching pad. Without his initiative and generosity, I would not have had the opportunity to build the business I loved for twenty-three years.

To my brother, Chuck Eigen, who, in October of 1987 during a brisk autumn nature walk through Wisconsin's famed Horicon Marsh, was first to suggest I write this book.

To Carole Stuart, Associate Publisher at Lyle Stuart and my editor, for her confidence in me and in this book.

To my good friend, Jim Wahner, whose support, clear thinking and crisp feedback contributed much to the shaping of my basic ideas.

To the many other executives with whom I discussed my ideas and who generously shared their professional experiences and personal beliefs. Among them, I want to give special thanks to: Tom Belfer, Ted Bruce, Carrie Delgado, Bill Domer, Winefred Johnson, Bill Johnston, Tom Keating, Bill Kraus, Jonathan Levine, Steve Mandelman, Peter McAvoy, Mary McCormack, Susan Mitchell, Alan Nemeth, Richard Pauls, Jim Shapiro, Kirby Shoaf, Toni Sikes, Richard Starich, John Teevan, John Uelmen and Don Vogel.

To my family and closest friends, Lynne and Russell Kagan, Bev and Mike Belfer, Jackie Blanchard, Mel Eck, Daryl and Carol Eigen, Dick and Wendy Eigen, Lou and Harriet Fine, Jerome Pashke, Colleen Poole, Tom Wittke, my son and daughter, Sam and Shayna, and my mother Pearl Eigen, whose enthusiastic cheerleading made this project doable and fun. And especially to my sister, Donna Wittke, for her long hours of editing.

And most important of all, to my wife, Diane, a remarkably perceptive woman without whose faith I would never have begun much less finished the project. Her patience and good humor encouraged me to keep writing when it sometimes seemed the entire English language had abandoned me. My sweet Diane, I thank you with all my heart, and I love you.

Contents

Introduction

It was October 1988, a couple of years after I sold my company. For more than two decades, I spent six days a week in the president's saddle and now it was over.

We began in September of 1963 in a single drug store. Well before the advent of Medicare, we were at the dawn of "home health care."

Starting as Sickroom Service, Inc., a name I later changed to HealthCall Corporation, we specialized in the rental and sale of medical equipment and supplies to patients at home. Though the bulk of our first year's business came primarily from our retail pharmacy, our focus and plans for future growth centered on the distribution of medical products to other retailers. The mainstay of our "durable" equipment inventory consisted of canes, crutches, wheelchairs, walkers, bathroom grab bars, hospital beds and traction devices. But we also carried dressings and catheters, elastic stockings and back supports, and numerous other types of "consumable" supplies used by patients after coming home from the hospital.

In time, we stocked nearly 10,000 different items from more than 500 manufacturers. Yet, while these products constituted the "stuff" of our business, they couldn't begin to define it. These were merely the products we bought and sold, the merchandise we carried, the inventory we warehoused and shipped to retailers who previously bought these same products directly from the manufacturer. We manufactured nothing. We were wholesalers and more often than not, especially in the early years, our prices were higher than the manufacturers' who for years were selling our customers direct.

Given the fact that our suppliers were also our competition, we knew we'd have to add value to the products we sold if our business had any chance of surviving. We'd have to give our wholesale customers something they weren't getting anywhere else. We'd have to give them service.

First, we designed an inventory control system for use by retail stores. Then we developed rental and sales policies and a billing system which allowed the retailer to stay abreast of renewal dates regardless of which day in the month a rental was initiated. We created snapout lease and sale forms in triplicate, which made the execution of transactions simple and fast. We organized both a retail and wholesale catalog bringing together many different products from hundreds of manufacturers in an organized, completely cross-indexed reference guide. We developed a training program which emphasized the fitting of equipment to the patient's disability rather than selection based upon what was in stock. Finally, we developed a full consignment program for durable medical equipment which gave our retailer customers the financing to operate like big stores even if they were small.

Over the next two decades we grew from that single drugstore to franchised outlets in 385 cities in 45 states, Puerto Rico and the U.S. Virgin Islands. We originated and hosted the largest Home Health Care Seminar and Exposition in the country which annually drew more than 2,500 people from all 50 states and Canada. We were featured in every major Pharmacy and Home Care journal in the country. And now, after 23 years of work and commitment, it was over.

I decided to take time, a month or two, to relax and enjoy the first extended vacation I'd had in a dozen years. My wife arranged a couple of small automobile trips. We took long walks together. I even went to an art supply store and bought paper and paint in an attempt to renew an old hobby. But, in spite of these diversions, I couldn't stop myself from thinking about the company—the company we'd started from scratch.

I thought about my 23 years in the trenches and kept asking myself what, if anything, I'd learned. I must have discovered some truths about business, about people. Was being in business really "one crisis after another," as a friend once defined it? Was it "more dealing with people than things" as a professor once cautioned? What worked? What mistakes could I have avoided? How could I have done things better?

My mind filled with images of employees—the wonderful and talented people who worked for us. I thought about the young ones, the older ones, the hundreds of men and women without whom we could never have existed. I knew many of them by name, from executives to truck drivers, from store managers to office workers, and now, I could still picture them clearly. There were Andrea Stevens and Will Callaghan. There were Jacob and Beverly and Kristin. There were Rita and Lou and Ray and Frank, and many, many unforgettable others. I remembered them as dedicated, honest, loyal people who truly cared about their jobs and about the company.

Without question, these employees were our company's most valuable resource. Most of them wanted our company to be successful. They wanted us to succeed, believing they could win promotions and make more money as a result. And yet, in spite of their good intentions, many of their dreams went unfulfilled. The truth was the majority of employees never advanced as they had hoped or prospered as they wished.

But, some employees were successful—the ones who were exceptionally effective. They were the heart and soul of our achievement, the reason for our success. They were the ones who grew steadily and prospered.

With the benefit of time and the advantage of hindsight, I began to realize that many of the good, hard working men and women who didn't succeed failed because they never really contributed in the way I wanted. That was the reason their potential went unrecognized and they didn't get the promotions they worked for.

I asked myself many questions. Why did some employees contribute so much and others so little? Why did so many, in spite of superior ability and talent, greater desire and deeper need, just plod along from day to day, from week to week, without ever fully understanding what their company was about? I knew they wanted to grow and get ahead, so why didn't more of them understand what I wanted? Why weren't they tuned in?

Now that I have some perspective and am away from the daily pres-

sure, I am able to see the difference between the employees who got
ahead and those who didn't. Our most successful employees shared
certain characteristics. They behaved in similar ways and shared common attitudes less successful employees had never learned. I could
begin to see a pattern emerging which helped to clarify why some got
promoted and others didn't.

Why hadn't I seen it sooner? If only I'd been bright enough to
understand all of this earlier, I would have done many things differently. I would have explained the strategy for success to every single
one of our employees, and done so every chance I got. Had I taken the
time or even thought of discussing this with our employees, more of
them would have performed in the way I wanted and, as a result, we
would have had a bigger, better and more profitable company. And I,
as a consequence, would have been a more successful boss.

I've compared notes with colleagues, other bosses who run companies of their own, and have confirmed that my experience was very
much like theirs. I learned other bosses want the same kinds of things
from their employees I wanted. And, like me, they rarely tell their
employees in straight, easy to understand language exactly what it is
they value. Rather, they expect their employees to come to work understanding intuitively what's required. It's as though we expect our
employees to read our minds.

The simple truth is we are wrong. Employees don't have ESP and
they can't know what's expected of them unless we tell them. They
can't get promoted unless we tell them how to get promoted, unless we
tell them why we promote people. That's why I decided to write this
book—to put on paper all the things I would have told our employees if
I knew then what I know now.

I would tell them that the secret of success is simple: Employees
who understand what their bosses want will be able to satisfy them,
and employees who satisfy their bosses will get promoted. I reasoned
that, not only would such a book benefit employees who want to move
up, it would benefit their bosses too. Employee success is, after all, in
the boss's interest because, ultimately, employee success is in the company's interest.

I wrote this book using my own experience and the experiences of
colleagues, so the situations and events described in the book are real.
Though many of the conversations actually happened, the characters
are fictional composites and any similarity between the individuals

depicted and actual persons is, therefore, unintentional and completely coincidental.

Now, before I go much further, I'd better add a word of caution. The ideas presented here are based on a number of important assumptions. I've made these assumptions because there are situations in which an employee can do little to improve his or her chances of getting promoted.

First, I have assumed all bosses are reasonable people. Unfortunately, as many employees know, this is not always the case. Some bosses are just plain unreasonable. And, while having a lousy boss does not make it impossible to get ahead, it can severely limit an employee's ability to get promoted. In Chapter 15, "What if Your Boss Is a Dud," I discuss strategies for overcoming a bad boss.

Second, I've assumed all bosses want their employees to behave in ways that will get them promoted. This, too, is not always true. Some bosses are living proof of the "Peter Principle" and have risen to positions beyond their abilities. These bosses may be easily threatened by ambitious employees and can dampen an otherwise enthusiastic promotion-getting effort.

Third, I've assumed every work environment is fertile ground for the ambitious. The truth is not every organization can or wants to encourage advancement. It may be the company is struggling and simply cannot afford to give raises and promotions. Or, the company's current management may be well established, entrenched, as is the case with some family-owned businesses. In those cases, there may be little or no opportunity for the development of new management positions and a career-minded employee may have little choice but to look elsewhere for growth opportunities.

And finally, I've assumed all people who read this book want to get ahead and move up in their companies. In other words, I've written the book for people who want a promotion. Now, certainly, there are many valuable employees who have no aspirations for larger roles in management, and that's fine. Not everybody can or should be climbing the corporate ladder.

But if you do want to move up—if you believe there are or could be opportunities for advancement in your company and want to do the things which can help you get promoted, read on. I've got something to say I think you really need to know.

HOW TO THINK LIKE A BOSS
And Get Ahead At Work

Chapter 1

Hard Work Won't Get You Promoted

Harry Porter sounded angry, but he was more scared than anything. Sitting there in the restaurant across the street from our office, he poured out his frustration to his friend and fellow employee, Gene Barton. "If I don't get what I want, I'm going to look for another job. That's all there is to it. No more mister nice guy. I've had it up to my eyebrows and I'm going to do something about it starting right now. I'll go through tonight's paper, I'll start circling the help wanted ads and . . ."

"Hold it, hold your horses," Gene interrupted. "What's the hurry?"

"I want a raise," Harry said, "and I want it now."

"Where's the fire, Harry? Give it a chance, a little time."

"I've been here for almost two years," Harry explained, "and I'm tired of not getting anywhere. Look at you. You're moving up. I want to get promoted and make more money too."

"These things don't happen easily, Harry. You've got to be patient."

"Patient?" Harry almost shouted. "I can't be any more patient. It's damn hard waiting around hoping your boss has plans for you and never knowing for sure what they are. I've got to know I have a future here. I can't keep slugging it out from day to day without knowing where it's leading."

Gene listened patiently, then he said simply, "Why don't you ask him?"

"I did," Harry answered. "I asked him about two months ago and he said something about things changing around here and opportunities in the future, but in the end what does it all mean? Nothing's changed."

"So, go and ask him again," Gene persisted.

"What for? He'll just keep treating me like a mushroom. That's what they've been doing you know, they've kept me in the dark and fed me manure."

"O.K., Harry, so you don't know what your potential is here—not yet, anyway. Now, as I see it, you've got a choice. You can drop everything and go looking for another job believing there's nothing for you here, or you can find out for sure before you throw away almost two years of getting yourself established. What have you got to lose? Go ask."

Harry stared into space.

"I'm asking you, Harry," Gene repeated. "What have you got to lose?"

Harry looked at his friend. His voice dropped softly. "O.K.," he said. "I'll ask again, but this better go somewhere or I'm out of here."

Several Days Later

It was 5:30 p.m. on a Friday afternoon. Harry Porter sat slumped in the chair in front of my desk, his hands unconsciously massaging each other as he struggled for the right words.

"I've been waiting for a chance to get promoted for almost two years now," he said. "I just don't understand why I'm not getting anywhere."

An assistant manager in data processing, Harry was a dependable, intelligent and conscientious employee who rarely missed a day's work. He was always reliable, solid, a family man. Everything about him spelled stability. While he had never received a promotion, Harry Porter was highly regarded in his department. He was an enthusiastic, hard worker who was respected by his supervisors and fellow employees alike. Most people would call him an ideal employee whom any boss would be proud to have on the payroll. One would think Harry Porter would be able to move along quickly, so why wasn't Harry moving up?

Sitting there in my office, Harry looked defeated. "I just want to know," he asked, "What does a person have to do around here to get a promotion?"

As president of my company for more than two decades, I've had the opportunity to face many Harry Porters. Some were men; some women. All were dedicated, loyal employees who shared the common belief that they had, by their loyalty and hard work, earned a promotion. Every last one of them earnestly believed he or she deserved to be promoted, or they believed at the very least they were entitled to a raise.

They said many of the same kinds of things. Some said their pay wasn't keeping up with inflation. Others pointed out they hadn't had a raise in a long time. Many explained they needed to make more money, and on and on. "George got a raise." "I'm working harder now than ever before." "I finished the assignment you gave me." "I have a friend who has the same kind of job I have and makes more than I do." And yet, these employees remained frustrated, unfulfilled and unpromoted, with only modest pay increases.

Many just seemed to be going through the motions, waiting for Fridays and holidays and vacations; the whole time wanting to get ahead but not really knowing how. They came to work, day after day, year after year, thinking they knew what to do and, yet, they were almost always completely off the mark.

On hearing his question that late Friday afternoon, I realized, in one respect at least, Harry Porter was different from many of the others. After all, Harry was there in my office asking the question most employees never ask: "What do I have to do to get a promotion?"

Many people think about their jobs. They think about their careers and ponder their futures, and wonder what it takes to get more responsibility, to get a chance at a bigger job, a crack at a promotion. Sometimes they ask their spouses, or they discuss it with friends and fellow employees, but they rarely ask their bosses. Imagine that. They rarely ask their bosses. One would think employees would ask them again and again simply because, if any one would know why he or she promotes people, it would be the boss. But, unlike Harry, most employees don't ask their bosses even though it's in their interest to do so.

It was on that Friday with Harry Porter I began to understand that my employees could never get ahead unless they shared my reality, my perspective. Unless they visualized our company's goals and measured its weaknesses and strengths as I did, how could they deal with its problems as I did? Unless they saw the world as I saw it, they couldn't hope to perform as I wanted them to perform. And if they didn't perform in ways satisfactory to me, why would I want to promote them?

Common Misconceptions About Getting Promoted

These employees shared the mistaken belief that getting ahead centered only around the quality of their performance at work. They believed the best way to get raises and promotions was to work hard and do a good job. They thought if they did their jobs extremely well, did the things they were asked to do, and did them with a minimum of error, their bosses would come to recognize their fine performance and reward them with raises and promotions. They believed raises and promotions were rewards for jobs well done. They thought it was that simple. They were wrong.

From my perspective, the idea that raises and promotions were rewards for lots of effort, hard work and good intentions had little or nothing to do with reality. Sure, like most bosses I gave routine raises at six and twelve month intervals to employees who performed as expected. But that wasn't why I gave the big raises, and it had nothing to do with why I gave important promotions. I gave the significant raises and promotions for altogether different reasons. They were intended to accomplish different purposes. My reality was different from the reality of most of our employees and that, I reasoned, was central to these employees' problems.

Now it is entirely possible that I'm wrong, that my perspective is faulty and my notion of what is good for the company is totally inaccurate. The question is: Does it matter whether I am right or wrong? Does it make any difference with respect to who gets a promotion? The undiluted truth is it doesn't make a bit of difference. Right or wrong, wise or stupid, the boss's view of reality is the only thing that determines who gets promoted. The boss's reality is the only reality that counts.

And yet, to their employees' detriment, most bosses don't share their reality with them. It's typically not a part of new employee orientation programs. It rarely shows up later in other kinds of in-service training programs. With rare exceptions, employers simply don't tell their employees how to get promoted. And without that training, without that essential information and understanding, employees cannot be expected to behave in promotable ways.

It was beginning to make solid sense—this thing about employees wanting to get ahead but not really doing the right things. I understood now that most employees didn't perform in ways that would encourage me to promote them because I never told them what I wanted. I never told them why I promote people. Thus I had to accept part of the responsibility for not giving them the information and the insight they needed.

So I looked across my desk at Harry Porter that Friday afternoon and said, "Harry, if you really want to get ahead in this organization—in any organization—here's what you've got to know."

"O.K.," he said enthusiastically. "I'm ready. This is what I need."

Universal Qualities That Turn Bosses On

Finish every day and be done with it. You have done what you could; some blunders and absurdities crept in; forget them as soon as you can. Tomorrow is a new day; you shall begin it well and serenely and with too high a spirit to be encumbered with your old nonsense.

—Ralph Waldo Emerson

"Let's begin with what I look for in the people I'm going to promote," I said. "I want people, Harry, with perspective, people with vision, people who can see the forest as well as the trees, people who can understand the long-term goals of the company and help us do things to reach those goals."

"Right," Harry responded, taking it in.

"I want people who will relieve me of some of the tasks I have to do," I continued. "That means I want people with initiative who will assume responsibility and carry through on a project as I would. I want people who can take a risk, people willing to make tough decisions, people who are not afraid to make mistakes. I don't want to answer every little question that comes up or follow the detail on every project. What I want is a little help, a little relief, some freedom to stand back from the detail so I can look at the broader picture."

I said I looked for people I could trust—not just people who were loyal—people who were honest. I said I wanted people who would let me know when they needed more information, people who were willing to say, "I don't know," and not pretend they do when they don't. I said I wanted executives who would own up to their responsibility for errors when they happened under their direction and credit those who report to them for achievement when they deserved credit. Trust in the people I promote, I said, was critically important, and honesty is the only way to establish trust.

I told him I looked for men and women who could be team players and team builders, people who could be leaders, people skillful in organizing and motivating others. I said half of any boss's job was facilitating others in their jobs. And what we needed, I said, were people who could stimulate others to be productive. Those were the people who could become our company's top managers.

I explained I wanted employees with the courage to say what they thought even when their thinking was contrary to my own. I valued debate, I said, and wanted people around me who would think for themselves and be willing to argue their position, stand up for what they believed in. But, I cautioned, I wanted employees who would be respectful of my experience and rank, offering criticism when it was appropriate—in private, never in public.

I was on a roll. It felt like I'd been carrying the burden of an undelivered speech.

I said I wanted people who could communicate orally and in writing—who could summarize issues and write opinions in succinct, easy to understand language. I wanted people with the ability to cut through the detail that usually surrounds an issue and get right to the heart of the matter—right to the point. Clarity, I said, is power, and I want people around me who are powerful, who write and speak understandably and with purpose. They are the ones who seem most able to get things done.

"Am I making sense, Harry?" I asked.

Harry stared at me and with an audible sigh, said, "Boy! You want a lot."

"Right you are, Harry," I told him. "I do want a lot. Promotions are not given easily, and they are not given just because people come to work and do a good job. When I hire people, I expect them to do a good job. I don't promote people for that."

He shifted uncomfortably in his chair. "Are you saying that working hard and doing your job well is not the way to get a promotion? Is that what I hear you saying?" he asked.

"I can tell you this, Harry," I said. "Hard work is important. Those who don't work hard virtually guarantee they won't get promoted. An employee has to do a good job to be in the running for a promotion, but that's a long way from saying that people get promoted *because* they work hard and do a good job. It's true, I won't promote someone who doesn't work hard. Hard work is an important prerequisite before I will consider the employee for a promotion, but I don't promote people for that alone."

If Harry had a light bulb over his head, it would have gone on right then. "So," he said, "It's something like a TV set. It has to be plugged in to work, but just because it's plugged in doesn't mean it will work."

"That's the idea, Harry. I don't promote people if they're not doing a good job, but doing a good job does not get someone promoted. I expect everyone to work hard and do a good job. That's what they're paid for. But, the important thing is this: the people who get promoted do more than a good job. They perform beyond expectations. And, they think in a certain way.

"The truth is, Harry, I promote people who think like a boss. What's more, I look for people who think like a boss before they get promoted. I don't want to give a promotion first and then sit back and hope the employee's performance rises to the occasion. That's a risk I don't want to take unless I have no choice. I want a safer route, as safe as possible. I want to know the employee will be able to handle the new job in advance. Then, I can give the promotion and not lose sleep over it."

Harry moved back into his chair to let the idea sink in.

"Here's the really important thing," I continued. "It's what motivates bosses to give promotions in the first place. Promotions and the bigger raises are given in order to get something. Bosses don't think of them as trophies for yesterday's accomplishments. They think of them as ways to reach tomorrow's goals. So, if the boss doesn't believe you'll be able to handle the new job, all the hard work in the world won't get you promoted."

He took a deep breath. I could see the wheels turning. "O.K.," he said. "I follow. But I'm wondering where I got the idea that promotions go to the people who work hard and do a good job. You know," he added, "I've thought that for as long as I can remember. And what's more, I know a lot of other people who think the same thing."

"Well, Harry," I went on, "I do understand that many people think of promotions as rewards for good behavior. They learned to think that from the time they were little. We all did. They learned those lessons as little kids and have carried them into adult life, and what they learned has kept them—is keeping them—from understanding the surest way to get ahead. So now, unfortunately, people who want to get promoted have to unlearn some of those things. They have to begin to see things in a new way, look at things from a new perspective."

There was a long pause. Finally he said, "If I hear you correctly, you're saying I'm not alone. You are making the point that a lot of people are tripping over their own feet because of what they learned when they were kids. I'd sure like to know what it is we learned that's holding us back, because I really do want to get somewhere in this company."

"O.K. Harry. Here's what I'd like to do. I'd like to share some stories with you about how different employees think and act, about what behavior works to the employee's benefit and what doesn't. And then, we can talk about what you have to know and how you have to think and what you have to do to get that promotion you want."

"Let's go," he said. "I couldn't be more ready."

*   *   *

Summary

Qualities that turn bosses on:

1. Vision—the ability to see the organization and its goals in total.
2. Initiative—the ability to get started on your own.
3. Risk Tolerance—the willingness to try new things even though you're not sure you will be successful.
4. Trustworthiness—this takes honesty and follow-through.
5. Confidence—enough to be able to say "I don't know," and "I made a mistake," and "Other people have good ideas too."
6. Leadership—the ability to motivate and direct others; the ability to build a team.
7. Courage—the willingness to think independently and stand up for your opinions.
8. Communication—the ability to write and speak clearly and succinctly.

Chapter 2

The "Be Good—Get Reward" Myth

God gives every bird its food, but He does not throw it into the nest.

—*J.G. Holland*

In the six months Janine Conrad was with us, she never ventured into my office. I exchanged occasional hellos with her in the employee lunchroom or as I passed her desk in the marketing department. Now, as she perched on the edge of the chair in front of my desk, she looked very uncomfortable indeed. This was the first time she had requested a meeting, and I knew why she was there. She was there to ask for a raise. I also knew it was a very difficult thing for her to do and guessed she had spent many hours practicing what she would say.

"I've been here six months," she began. "I do my job very well. I'm dependable and only missed work twice when my kids were sick. I understand that reviews come at about six months, so I'm here . . . I'm here to ask for a raise."

Over the years, I must have had 500 similar requests for raises. Of those 500, a half dozen or so have been what I considered persuasive presentations. The other 494 were some version of: "I deserve a raise because I've been here for a reasonable period of time" or, " . . . because I've mastered my job" or, " . . . because I come in on time and do exactly what I'm told" or, " . . . because I never make mistakes" or, " . . . because I want to buy a house or have a baby" or, " . . . because so-and-so makes more than I do," and dozens of similar reasons.

None of the above arguments have much to do with why people get raises, yet hundreds of people have asked for raises using those very words. Most people based their requests on the fact that they were "good"—good at their jobs, good followers of orders, good hard working people who obeyed the rules and did exactly what was expected of them.

What baffled me most over the years, especially about younger employees, was the overwhelming number of folks who expected to be rewarded for reaching a target on the calendar. They also believed that just getting to the point where they could do their jobs adequately was justification for an increase in pay. There was an expectation that just doing the job and being around for six months or so entitled them to a raise. And when they mastered the jobs for which they were hired, they were absolutely certain they were entitled to make more money.

My thinking was different. I knew when I hired someone that the company would have to endure the time and expense of training the employee. I could accept that because it was part of the cost of doing business, but I thought, when a new employee finally got to the point where he or she was able to do the job, it would be appropriate for the company to recover the expenses of training before it gave a raise. I've since learned a lot of bosses believe the same thing.

The problem is most of us have been indoctrinated with the idea that life provides rewards for jobs well done. It's part of the work ethic, pure and simple—you work hard and you get rewarded. It's a lesson we all learned as children. I'm no different. I learned it too.

My father was a letter-winning tight end for the University of Wisconsin football team and had always wanted me to succeed in the game. So I became a halfback on my high school team. In the evening, my dad would tell heroic stories about his own gridiron days, and he'd coach me with great tips like, "Mix it up. Catch 'em off guard. First, fake right and go left; then fake right and go right."

I tried very hard, but when you're running with the ball and a Neanderthal with no neck and webbed thighs is lumbering toward you, it's damn hard to remember which combination of fakes is up next. I struggled to make him proud of me, yet it became increasingly clear that the prospects of my becoming a football star were dim indeed. My father, however, would not be denied. He came to every game undaunted, hoping for heroism, praying for the impossible.

Then, one cold November day I did it. It was late in the fourth quarter. My team was behind by three points. It was third down and goal to go, and I got the call. "Hut, hut, hut," the quarterback barked and the ball was snapped. I took the ball on a quick hand-off and plunged over tackle for the one and only touchdown of my high school career. Not until years later did I ever tell anyone that I did it with my eyes shut.

The locker room was bedlam after the game. People were shouting and singing and celebrating our victory all over the place. My dad was in the stands that day and I knew he would be waiting for me. I could hardly wait to see him myself. I showered, dressed and hurried to the parking lot where he was waiting in the family car.

"That's my boy!" he cheered when he saw me. "That's my boy!" We talked and joked and laughed all the way home. It was undoubtedly one of the best drives I ever had with my father. What a memory.

For the many afterschool scrimmages, stuffy locker rooms and uninspiring chalkboard lectures, my father's genuine approval that day made it all worthwhile. It was the only reward I needed and, at a conscious level, I always knew that's why I played football.

Actually, I started learning the reward system long before my football days. "Be a good boy," my mother used to say, "and I'll bake your favorite cookies." "If you mow the lawn," my dad would say, "you can use the family car this weekend." It's the BE GOOD—GET REWARD lesson, and we learn it in one form or another throughout our childhoods. It's a lesson that is learned and reinforced, time after time, in a thousand and one ways.

Parents reward their children with allowances on the condition they keep their rooms tidy. High school and college students everywhere know the reward for regular study will be good grades, and good grades, we're promised, will be rewarded with a good job. Even Christmas presents are sometimes described as rewards for being good. You "better be good," we're told in the popular Christmas song, because, "Santa Claus is coming to town," and, "he knows if you've been naughty or nice." And when we're older, our religious leaders proclaim that heaven is the reward for living a saintly life. The BE GOOD—GET REWARD message is everywhere. Even convicts get time off for good behavior.

Is it any wonder that most Americans come to their jobs and professions believing that the way to get ahead is by being obedient, following the rules, doing what we are told and working hard? Is it surprising that employees work at their jobs thinking of promotions as the rewards for doing their jobs well?

People learn as children to expect rewards for being "good" but, where promotions on the job are concerned, "good" isn't good enough. Bosses want something more. Bosses come to the game expecting their employees to perform well. They aren't impressed by employees who meet basic standards—they're impressed by those who exceed them.

The BE GOOD—GET REWARD lesson is a good lesson for kids, but it's the wrong lesson for adults who want to be promoted. Bosses give promotions and raises for other reasons entirely. Bosses never promote people because they were effective yesterday—bosses promote people because they expect them to be effective tomorrow.

Bosses Are Human Too

Most bosses should and do care about their employees' welfare and want them to do well. But, perhaps simply because bosses are human, their employees' needs don't always come first. Bosses have good days, bad days, problems at work, children to raise, bills to pay and dreams to pursue. Just like employees, bosses have dozens of things in their lives begging for their attention. In addition, bosses must always be concerned with the prosperity of the enterprise. That is the crucial part of the boss's world. Problems arise when the worlds of boss and employee are far apart.

Your boss may be able to share your world a glimpse at a time, but for the most part, your boss has to live in his or her own world, has to deal with his or her own problems. What this means when it's promotion time is if the boss's needs and the employee's needs have to vie for first place on the agenda, you know whose are going to come first.

Promotions: Solutions to Tomorrow's Problems

Bosses see job vacancies as problems they have to solve. They look at their employees and try to identify those who can provide solutions to those problems. The hard truth is promotions are not given to reward good employees, they are given to solve the boss's problems. They are given to make the boss's life easier.

Promotions and, in one respect, even the most routine of raises are given because the boss is gambling that the employee's performance will provide a payback down the road. The boss is not paying for past achievements. The boss is betting on the future.

Employees who think a raise is justified because they've put in six months or so couldn't possibly understand what their bosses really want. Routine raises never provide an incentive for excellence, and most bosses know that. Maybe the perception that raises and promotions are given as rewards for past achievement arises from the fact that, at the time a raise or promotion is given, many bosses cite good things the employee has done in the past. Or, it may arise because most employees know they can expect modest raises from time to time just by staying around and performing at minimally acceptable levels.

If bosses know that routine raises are not bets on future excellence, why do such raises in many organizations continue to be routine? The long and short of it is that routine raises are given because it has become custom. They have become part of our culture and bosses understand that not giving annual and semi-annual raises is certain to be interpreted by some employees as punitive. So, we give these routine bumps in order to avoid giving the wrong impression.

Yet, in spite of the fact that we give routine raises to accommodate the culture, we also give them with the clear, calculated expectation of a future payoff. We give them to get something. At a bare minimum, we are gambling the employee will stick it out a little longer and not start looking for another job.

The fact remains, major raises and important promotions occur only when they are "boss beneficial," not when they are exclusively "employee beneficial." They occur when the boss believes the employee is important to the company's future. Those which benefit the employee alone stand almost no chance of occurring. These are the hard cold facts. It may not seem fair or nice, but if you face the truth, you can operate in ways that will help you get ahead.

The key lesson for employees is this: Know for a fact, when a promotion is being considered the major question the boss will be asking is . . .

HOW WILL PROMOTING THIS PERSON HELP ME?

* * *

Summary

1. Stop thinking of raises and promotions as rewards for good work. Bosses expect their employees to perform well. They aren't impressed by employees who meet basic standards—they're impressed by those who exceed them.

2. Promotions are not given as medals for past or even present achievements, they are given in the hope the employee's performance will provide a payback down the road. They are given with the expectation of future performance.

3. Understand that raises and promotions are given to solve the boss's problems and make the boss's life easier.

4. Raises and promotions occur only when the boss views the employee's welfare as tied directly to the welfare of the company and, therefore, tied to his or her own welfare.

5. When a promotion is being considered, the major question the boss will be asking is: "How will promoting this person help me and the company?"

6. Prepare for a raise request by listing the contributions you can make to the company tomorrow, not just what you did yesterday.

Chapter 3

How Powerful People Win Promotions

Rashness is the characteristic of ardent youth, and prudence that of mellowed age.

—Cicero

Right after lunch, Rita Wilson flew into my office and threw herself into the chair across from my desk. "I've had it up to here," she puffed. "If you don't do something about those idiots in shipping, you can find someone else to handle the phones. I'm ready to quit."

Rita managed one of five CRT telephone order stations in our customer service department, and for weeks she had been besieged by calls from unhappy customers who were complaining about incorrect shipments.

"I swear," Rita continued, "that guy George and the rest of his crew are 'on' something. They just can't keep the orders straight, and we're the ones who have to handle all of the phones. Our customers are hotter'n pistols, and I can't say I blame them. Somebody better straighten George out. I don't know how many shipments have gone out wrong that we still haven't found out about. You've got to do something!"

It took several minutes to calm her down. Finally she said, "It's just no fun working here anymore. I used to enjoy coming to work. But lately, it seems all we do is put out fires. I hate it!"

"I know the feeling," I told her. "None of us likes it when our days are filled with problems."

"For weeks now," Rita confessed, "I just wake up with dread about having to come to work in the morning."

"It will be O.K., Rita. I'll get over to the shipping area within the hour and see what's up. In the meantime, why don't you take a few minutes to relax before you go back to work. I'll let you know what I find out."

Rita thanked me, and as she was leaving my office she turned and said, "I'm really sorry I burst in on you like that. It's just been so awful, and I feel like there isn't anything I can do about it. Sorry."

"Everything will be all right," I assured her. "You go take a few minutes off now and I'll talk to you later." She left my office and headed down the hall.

I tried to maintain an "open door" policy in our company whenever possible. To our employees it meant that, unless I was in a meeting, anybody could walk into my office at any time and unload. A number of employees did just that over the years, and I've been told it was comforting to know my door was open should they ever feel the need.

Rita Wilson felt the need about every other month. And she always got what she came for—a little comfort, a little reassurance, and a sense that "Dad" would take care of everything and make it, whatever it was, all O.K. again.

While Rita always got what she came for, she reinforced a message about herself every time she burst into my office. The message said, "I am a little kid." It was a message in which she declared, "The adult world is a very scary place, especially here at work, and I want the company to take care of me. I don't want to be the one who takes care of things. I just want to come to work and have everything go O.K. I want my life to be free of problems. I want to enjoy my job."

There is, of course, considerable risk in assuming responsibility for one's successes and failures. It's much safer to let someone else be responsible for what we can or cannot achieve. It's safer to give the power away. "It's their fault," some say. "It's not my job." "It's all politics." "It's not what you know, it's who you know." "I was just doing what I was told." "My boss doesn't like me." All these are affirmations that the employee has no power, no control.

When Rita was little, big people had all the power and she needed their permission for almost everything. And now, in spite of the fact that she had grown up and become an adult, Rita operated as though she were nine years old; she still believed the big people at work had all the power. Without realizing it, Rita wanted the company to be her family. She related to me in much the same way she used to relate to her parents. To Rita, I became a kind of surrogate father.

Bosses, however, are not like parents. While parents willingly make sacrifices on behalf of their children, most bosses don't. Employers do care about their employees and want them to succeed and be happy in their jobs, but their first priority is to improve the prosperity of the enterprise. They become concerned with the prosperity of their employees second. It's a natural and necessary order and all bosses know it. They know that without a financially healthy organization, employee prosperity is simply not possible.

Employees who adopt "little kid" positions have a difficult time understanding that, from the boss's point of view, the company must come first. They behave in ways that say, "Please take care of me," and by doing so, they effectively communicate to their bosses that they are not ready for more responsibility, which means they are not ready for a promotion. After all, the boss is looking for people who will help solve the company's problems—not be part of the problem.

"Little kid" positions can be very subtle. I recall a particular staff meeting in which Fred, Donna, Robert and Edward, four of our regional sales managers, were discussing the resignation of the fifth, Chuck Pendleton. In seven years with the company, Chuck had been a very effective and highly visible sales executive. He called on fifty of our top wholesale accounts and had, over time, developed excellent working relationships with all of them. Now he was leaving to take a job in Connecticut, the state he called "home."

The reason for the meeting was to discuss how Chuck's departure would impact our future business with his old customers. Fred was the first to speak. "We've got to remember," he said, "our customers really liked working with Chuck. And since we want them to feel O.K. about his not being here any more, I think we should send out an announcement that downplays Chuck and focuses instead on the merits of his replacement."

Robert, who sat directly across from Fred at the meeting, spoke next. "We all know, Fred, that you're taking over Chuck's territory. Don't you think it's a little self-serving to want the announcement to focus on you?"

"Not at all," Fred shot back. "The whole idea is to help Chuck's customers warm up to their new account executive. Even if it does help me," he argued, "it helps the company too."

Donna had been listening to the exchange between Fred and Robert. Finally, she put her palms on the conference table as if to take charge of the conversation and said, "I think it makes perfect sense to change the customer's focus from Chuck to Fred. My only concern has to do with how Chuck is treated in the announcement. I'm afraid anything less than a positive statement about Chuck might be interpreted by his old customers as sour grapes on the part of the company. And I don't think that will help Fred or the company one bit."

"I don't know," Robert complained. "I think somebody ought to write a complimentary memo about us and send it to our customers. I don't think it's fair to just give Chuck a big buildup. He's gone, after all. We're all still here, and I don't see anybody writing complimentary memos about us."

Donna ignored his comment. "If it's O.K. with everyone," she offered, "I'll do the first draft of the memo. Then, when I'm finished, you can all have a go at it and do whatever editing you think is necessary." Fred loved having Donna relieve him of the initial work and accepted her offer gladly. Edward, always quiet, nodded his approval. Robert also agreed, though he made it very clear to everyone he did so with reluctance.

This simple exchange illustrates the kinds of roles employees sometimes assume. Donna consistently acted as an adult "big sister" or "mother." She was often consulted by other employees to mediate disputes or simply to unload a personal or work related problem. Because she was able to stay adult and rational in most situations, her value to the company increased.

Edward, Robert and Fred all suffered from varying degrees of "little kidism." Edward usually went along with the crowd. Because he was unwilling to express a real opinion or disagree with me or his colleagues in any meaningful way, his value decreased. Fred was probably the kind of kid who always grabbed the biggest piece of cake for himself, and Robert was the one who went running to mom to tell on Fred. While both these managers had many wonderful qualities that made them valuable to the company, they held themselves back by being kids when they should have been adults.

Among the four, Donna was the first to get promoted. In due time, Fred's and Edward's promotions followed when they learned to "grow up" and take on more and more responsibility. Robert's position did not improve and he resigned within two years.

The Roles Employees Play

Each day, in offices and factories all over the country, people assume different roles. Their ages notwithstanding, many employees operate from "little kid" positions. Look around; you'll recognize a lot of them. There's the "It's not my job" position. This is often just another version of "I did the dishes last night, mom. It's Sally's turn to do them tonight."

Then, there's the "There's nothing to do" position. I can't tell you how many times I've been approached by employees with the "What should I do now?" look, as though I am the only one with a grip on the big picture. It's reminiscent of the little kid who makes the bed just like mommy said, but doesn't hang up his clothes until "mommy" gives the next command. Adults who want to get ahead think for themselves and anticipate the needs of the organization. They don't just complete the assigned task and then wait for further direction.

There's the "I don't know how" position. When my son was three years old, he knew how to dress himself perfectly well, but he would manipulate his mother into dressing him morning after morning by insisting he didn't know how. Sometimes employees hold themselves back because, like my son at three, they are afraid to accept new responsibilities and try new things.

There's the "Pay attention to me" position. Have you ever tried to have a conversation with an adult while your five-year-old interrupted incessantly to capture your attention? Sometimes in staff meetings, otherwise very grown-up executives will use every opportunity to make a point in order to bring attention to themselves regardless of how timely or appropriate the point. This is a tricky issue because bosses applaud employees who are willing to contribute in meetings, a behavior to be valued and cultivated. Perhaps the question is, "Have you something new to offer, or are you simply talking to be talking?"

For me, the most objectionable slip into "little kid" is the "I didn't do it" position. When I was a kid and broke the vase on the dining room table, our Irish Setter was banned from the house for three days until I finally confessed. Behavior like that is tolerable in children. In adults, however, it signals dishonesty and insecurity—two qualities which will always eliminate an employee's prospects for advancement. Bosses value people who are adult enough to own up to their failures, not just their successes.

My message to employees who want to get ahead is straightforward and simple: Little kids don't win promotions. Bosses promote people who exhibit adult responsibility and control, think for themselves, solve problems and help get things done.

Power Is the Expectation of Success

Suppose on that day after lunch when Rita Wilson came into my office, she had come not only with a problem, but with a solution—and had, instead, said something like this:

"Have you got a minute? I'd like to discuss something with you. We've got a real problem in our shipping department. That guy, George, and his crew are making far too many mistakes. I'm getting calls from our customers reporting that they're getting other people's shipments in place of their own. Understandably, they're upset. So here's what I think we ought to do.

"In a nutshell, George and his people need some retraining. I've already talked with him, and I think I've identified what it is they're not understanding about our system. I also think that, since George's people have to read the shipment orders our department generates, it makes perfect sense for me to be communicating with them.

"So, what I'm asking from you is authorization to spend an hour or two in a training session with George and his crew. If I can do that, I think we will fix the current problem and establish a pattern for communication that will enable us to more routinely discuss problems that may develop in the future."

Wow! What a difference. If that had been Rita Wilson's original approach, not only would she have taken the bull by the horns by first having a preliminary discussion with George, but she would have come to my office with a plan for doing something. And she would have come with an understandable rationale for her plan of action as well as a pretty good analysis of how to handle future problems with George. Had Rita Wilson come into my office that day with a solution instead of a problem, she would have instantaneously made herself a prime candidate for promotion.

This second Rita Wilson, you'll agree, is a powerful person. Powerful people believe they are responsible for themselves, and that they can affect their futures in direct and positive ways. Accordingly, they exert effective influence in their work environments with the full expectation that they can improve themselves in their careers. Powerful people get ahead.

Acting "As If"

I've given hundreds of speeches over the years and yet, like most people, I still get nervous before I address a group of people. Even professional speakers, I'm told, get stage fright now and then. It's normal. My fear has lessened over time, but I'll never forget my first major talk to a large professional audience. I had been invited by N.A.R.D., the National Association of Retail Druggists, to speak to its annual convention. Pharmacists from all over the country came to attend workshops, seminars and lectures on the current practice of Community Pharmacy, and I was asked to speak about the efficacy and future of home health care.

I was young, and I was scared. About 800 people were in the audience that afternoon and, as I recall it, there were no real people, just a mass of suits and dresses that blended into a hazy blur before me. I have trouble remembering exactly what I said in that speech, but I'll never forget how I felt as I walked to the lectern.

I was scared. I stood there, gripping the podium with both hands, happy it was there to hide my shaking knees. It was hot. My brow was dripping. I used my thumb like a squeegee to wipe the sweat running into my eyes and prayed no one would notice how uncomfortable I really was. My mouth became dry—dryer than dry. My tongue felt like cardboard. I wanted to reach for a glass of water but none was in sight.

Then I got a horrifying thought: My mouth was so dry the right side of my upper lip was going to get permanently stuck to my teeth and I'd have to go through the entire speech with this ridiculous twisted smile. The audience wouldn't be able to tell if I was having fun or in pain. My God, I thought, I just want out of here.

As I think back, that speech must have gone well because the N.A.R.D. invited me to speak several times in the years that followed—or maybe its administrations changed and the new people didn't know how bad I was. It never fails, however, even these days. Whenever I'm preparing for a speech, making notes and drafting outlines, I get nervous, I feel those familiar butterflies in my stomach, my mouth gets dry and I get the same, horrifying thought that, in the middle of my speech, my lips will stick to my teeth.

Over the years, speaking in public has taught me an important lesson. Audiences never really know how nervous I am—as long as I act as if I am confident and enjoying myself. That's the important part: *Act as if.* Audiences don't want to sit in front of a nervous speaker. They want the speaker to enjoy speaking and appear as though he or she just loves being there to speak to them. So, as long as I come to the podium with energy and a smile and look like I really enjoy being there, they can never tell how nervous I am. I act as if I'm not nervous and you know what? It works. Before I realize it, I am no longer nervous.

Act as if. When you've had a bad day, and we all have bad days, act as if things are going handsomely—even if they're not. When you are on the road making a tough sales call, act as if you really enjoy talking to that customer about your company and its products—even if you don't. When you are talking to your boss about your company's problems and your ideas for solving them, act as if you are perfectly comfortable discussing them with people at his or her level—even if you're not. That is power, and powerful people get promoted.

It's easy to recognize powerful people. They are comfortable and relaxed in social settings, and they are all business when they are at a task. They dress as conservatively as the top executives in their firm, carry themselves with confidence and speak with purpose. Their voices are controlled; they rarely shout. Their speech is measured, minimal and always to the point. They are clear and easy to understand. They seem to know that clarity is power. And, perhaps most important, they talk about how to get things done assuming what they talk about will work. They believe in their own effectiveness. They get things done because they focus on the "how to," not on the "what if."

Powerful, however, does not mean overbearing or heavy handed. And it doesn't mean dictatorial. Powerful means in control, in charge and responsible. It means reliable, steady and solid. Powerful people make excellent candidates for promotion because bosses want strong people with whom they can share responsibility. Bosses want people they can trust, people who will get the job done on time, on budget and in a manner which will never detract from the organization's image with its various publics.

Power is more a matter of attitude than authority. It is optimism and purpose combined. People with power are goal oriented and always seem to have something to do. And when they do it, they flavor their efforts with spirit and zest. They are high-energy doers who know how to have fun while they get things done.

Powerful people go about their business with the expectation of success, a visible attitude of achievement and an air of accomplishment that no one can miss. A powerful attitude breeds confidence and security in other employees and, most important, in those to whom the employee reports. Powerful people inspire others to action. Bosses want powerful people around them, people who help create an environment for winning. Powerful people get promoted. Kids never do.

*   *   *

Summary

1. Bosses promote powerful people.
2. Bosses promote people who think for themselves and anticipate the needs of the organization.
3. Bosses promote people who carry themselves with confidence and speak with purpose.
4. Bosses promote people who are comfortable in social settings, yet are all business when they are at a task.
5. Bosses promote people who are goal oriented and always seem to have something to do.
6. Bosses promote people who will help solve the company's problems, people who come with solutions instead of problems.
7. Bosses promote people who are willing to take more responsibility and accept more work.

Chapter 4

Why Perfect Employees Go Nowhere

Bachelor's wives and old maid's children are always perfect
—Chamfort

The need to be perfect is sometimes hammered into us from the time we're tots. We learn to color within the lines, do exactly what we're told and be good. This message can be so strong it can inhibit us from learning how to think for ourselves, take risks and trust our own instincts. Our creativity can be stunted. We can become overly cautious and fearful of making mistakes. We can learn to believe that the fewer mistakes we make, the better we'll do our jobs and the faster we'll get ahead. We can learn to strive for perfection.

Beverly Trent is an excellent example. Beverly worked in our Accounts Payable department for six years—maybe more. She was always punctual, extremely conscientious and meticulously accurate. She was, in short, a steady employee who everyone agreed was just about perfect at her job, and yet each year she only got the usual modest raises.

The truth is Beverly was a valuable employee. Even she knew it. But she also knew she was not getting ahead in the way she wanted. She felt stuck in her job. It had become routine and she was bored. Still, she came to work every day and performed so well and so cheerfully it never occurred to anyone that what she wanted was a job with more responsibility and more pay.

Beverly Trent had bought into the BE GOOD—GET REWARD belief system to such an extent she could only conclude that some failure, some inadequacy, some imperfection in her performance was responsible for holding her back. She wasn't getting ahead, she reasoned, because she wasn't as perfect in her job as she should have been. She thought she had to do better. Yes, yes, that was it. She would try harder, work longer, change something. More education, she decided, would solve the problem.

First she went to the library. She studied books on time management and self-motivation. She read magazine articles on office systems and communication. Then, she signed up for a night school class in computer literacy, enrolled in a correspondence course in business writing and, finally, took a weekend seminar in office organization—all designed to win her the long-desired promotion. Sadly, it never came.

When Perfection Backfires, It's Suicide

What Beverly didn't know is that job perfection can backfire and keep a person stuck in the position he or she has mastered. Here's how: Let's suppose a position opens in the company and the boss responsible for filling it prefers to promote from within. Suppose further the boss has identified an employee who has all the skills to handle the new job. Making such a promotion should be a relatively uncomplicated matter, even automatic. A promotion, however, is never automatic, and is never considered in a vacuum.

Promotions from within set up a chain reaction in which the first one leads to a series of lesser ones, each intended to fill the vacancies of the people promoted in front. The boss must think through how and by whom the employee's old responsibilities will be handled after the promoted employee leaves the old job. If Beverly is promoted, who is going to take her place? Her assistant? If so, then who will replace her assistant? And so on.

So, if the employee being considered for promotion is spectacularly good at the current job, finding a good replacement will be that much harder. More effort will be needed in the search and interview process and more training will be required. In this sense, the cost to the organization when an excellent employee is promoted is greater than when an ordinary employee is promoted. So, because it's more difficult and also more costly, employees who are exceptionally good at their jobs may have a harder time getting promoted if the boss has other options available. Sometimes, perfection acts like glue. The better an employee is, the stickier the current job becomes. No one wants to replace an already perfect employee because, if it works, why fix it?

What employees need to understand is that excellence in the current job is never enough. They must demonstrate either that their skills are transferable to a bigger job, or that they are capable of learning to handle a bigger job. The key is this: Exceptionally good employees get promoted only when the boss believes the promotion will provide greater benefits to the company—not to reward the employee for excellence. To be promoted, the employee must be perceived as more valuable in the new job than in the old.

It's O.K. Not to Know Everything

There is another problem for employees who strive for perfection. It is believing that only total perfection will impress the boss. This employee believes it isn't enough to merely perform well. He or she must appear to be perfect in every respect.

Perfect people, however, aren't believable. The president of a large, national company, shares my perspective. He told me about turning down an otherwise perfectly qualified job candidate simply because the candidate was, in his words, "groomed too meticulously."

"I think good grooming is important," he explained, "but this guy was so perfect he was scary. His clothes were perfect. His shoes were perfect. His hair was perfect. His fingernails were perfect. His tan was perfect. His actions were controlled and his voice was deep and modulated. Even his teeth were perfect. Everything about him was perfect. He was plastic, and I don't trust that in anybody." He added, "Nobody is perfect!"

"Nobody's perfect." Sounds real, doesn't it? It is real. You know it and bosses know it too. The "always perfect" employee scares bosses—not because they are threatening, but because they don't seem real, and artificial people are hard to trust.

Unfortunately, too many people get the notion that if the boss sees a few imperfections, the chances for promotion will evaporate. These folks waste a lot of energy trying to hide their imperfections. They guard their speech, avoid giving criticism, sit in the back row at meetings and stay as inconspicuous as possible for fear they will slip along the way and reveal the horrible truth—that they are not perfect after all.

My observation was that people rarely hid it well. Usually, the first clue was the smiling, silent, affirmative nod when given any kind of direction, no matter how complicated. This artificially confident nod always seems to me like the employee was saying, "What? Not understand your directions! Me? No way! What do you think, I'm some kind of dummy? Say listen, boss, I want you to know I understood what you were saying almost before you said it."

It is a behavior reminiscent of classroom students who never raise their hands; who never say, "I don't know." Talking to employees who remain silent, who nod vague affirmations, who never risk a question or comment, and who never—I mean never—say, "I don't know," is frustrating. There's no give and take, no feedback, no real communication. All the employee's energy is put into maintaining a facade.

It is unproductive behavior, really—first, because it prevents the employee from getting the information needed to perform well, and second, because bosses, like teachers, know better. In my own company I should have grabbed a megaphone and announced: "Attention all employees who want to be promoted—It's O.K. to say, 'I don't know.'"

If only all employees could listen to private conversations between corporate executives at the highest levels, they would frequently hear the phrase, "I don't know." Even in the board room, it's O.K. to indicate one doesn't know everything. It's routine for top executives to say, "I don't know," and "That's over my head," and "I need to get up to speed on this," and "Run that by me again."

No one knows everything, and behavior which attempts to present a flawless image is always a dead giveaway for what it really is: a very high degree of personal insecurity. Such behavior evidences uncertainty, it suggests weakness and reveals the employee is misinformed about what bosses truly want in the employees they promote.

Bosses are not looking for people who already know everything about the job, because those people don't exist. Bosses are looking for people who can do the job because they have the necessary talents, the necessary skills, the motivation, curiosity, risk-tolerance and, most important, the willingness to think.

Bosses want people who ask questions until they get the information they need. They know that nobody knows everything, especially in a new job. Bosses know it requires time to "get up to speed." They want people around them who are willing to explore new options and try new things. They want people willing to laugh at themselves and let their hair down once in a while. In other words, bosses want real human beings in their organizations.

The Joy of Making Mistakes

Imagine your boss stopping you in the hall and saying something like this: "The problem with you, Tony, is you never make mistakes. And since you don't make mistakes, I can't even begin to think of promoting you. It's as simple as that. In other words, Tony, if you want to get ahead in this organization, you'd better start making some mistakes and you'd better start making them right now."

Sounds ridiculous, doesn't it? After all, don't most people think bosses want nothing to do with employees who make mistakes? Don't most people think the only way to get ahead is to not make mistakes? Not making mistakes is, after all, just another way of saying the employee is doing good work—and we've all been raised on the BE GOOD—GET REWARD belief system.

I want to clarify that making mistakes has no value of its own. Nobody wants employees to make mistakes. But reasonable bosses know that mistakes are part of the process of learning, part of the experience of exploration and risk taking. They are the unavoidable cost of entering new territory. Stupid mistakes, however, are something else. Bosses don't value mistakes which result from inattention to detail and sloppiness, and they don't appreciate it when yesterday's mistakes are repeated. All bosses expect their employees to think.

The point is that bosses want their employees to explore the limits of their jobs in the hope they will discover new and better ways of doing things. Bosses want that because it's the only way an organization can stay fresh, the only way an organization can get better. And, bosses know that anyone who risks trying new things is certain to make a mistake here and there. It's the price of doing what we're not used to doing. It goes with the territory.

When mistakes are made, there is a right way and a wrong way to handle them. The wrong way is to hide your mistakes. The right way is to "fess up," tell those who will be affected by your mistakes so they can avoid the consequences or minimize the damage. Tell everyone who might be affected and I guarantee they will appreciate your effort to help them avoid further difficulty. When you do this, they will be more apt to forgive you for your mistakes, knowing that everyone makes them.

The only way to avoid making mistakes is to never do anything new. From my point of view, the very fact that an employee never makes mistakes is evidence that creativity is at a standstill. It suggests the employee is immersed in the details of the day-to-day job and is not thinking in the future.

If the employee is not looking to the future, how can the boss even begin to think of his or her potential for leadership? How can the boss be confident in the employee's ability to forestall upcoming problems, anticipate tomorrow's challenges and provide future leadership? Employees who operate with one foot in the future by trying new things will make mistakes. Yet, with the obvious exception of jobs that require absolute accuracy, these are the employees most likely to get promoted. Employees who play it safe and avoid making mistakes are doomed to go nowhere.

I wish I would have routinely said to my employees, "Go ahead, Take a few risks. Try doing some new things. Explore the frontiers. Come up with something new. Give us an edge. Make us different. Make us better. And if you make a few mistakes along the way, so be it. It's one of the costs of innovation. It's the price of creativity. We'll pay for a few mistakes because we know it's much more costly to do nothing. Because when we do nothing, it is impossible to improve. If necessity is the mother of invention, then mistakes are its offspring. Go invent!"

Enough Is Enough

Sometimes perfection-conscious employees don't get the job finished because it's never perfect enough. This often results in delays that can cause problems in other areas of the organization. Remember Rita Wilson's issue with the shipping department? When employees in that department first learned there were numerous shipping errors, reactions were mixed.

Those on the first shift refused to take responsibility for any of the errors. They had worked very hard at not making mistakes. When they filled orders, they were extremely careful about the merchandise they picked and just as careful about packing, weighing and shipping those orders. They knew they handled each order with consummate care, and they were certain the mistakes couldn't be theirs.

So they blamed the second shift. Later analysis seemed to substantiate their claim showing that, in fact, the vast majority of shipping errors did occur during the second shift. Yet, without realizing it, the first shift was in part responsible for the errors created by the second.

Because the first shift's work was carefully meticulous and, therefore, methodically slow, they never quite finished their normal allotment of orders. Their careful work resulted in a stack of unfilled orders that were left each day for the start of the second shift. When this daily backlog was added to the normal allotment of second-shift orders, it created an immense amount of work for the second shift. Pressured by the weight of this inherited backlog, the second shift was forced to rush just to get the orders out. Not surprisingly, shipping errors multiplied.

Perfection-seeking causes delays, and delays cause problems. Unfortunately, problems caused by "perfect" employees can occur anywhere. Sales managers can let the iron get cold while they double-check discounts and make certain their bids have all the "T's" crossed and all the "I's" dotted. Public relations people can polish their copy until the story gets cold. Purchasing managers can get so focused on new products they ignore stock-out emergencies in bread and butter inventories. Sales clerks can concentrate so intently on the customers in front of them that they ignore other customers waiting for service.

There are times when you've just got to "Get while the gettin's good," and that means get the job done; not perfect, just done. If you miss your deadlines, no amount of perfection will matter. If you focus too intently on one aspect of your job you lose sight of others, no level of perfection will be sufficient.

Sometimes, an emphasis on quality can be a disguise for procrastination. If you find yourself reviewing and polishing and checking and researching, stop and ask yourself, "What's really going on here? Am I avoiding getting started, or worse, am I avoiding getting finished?"

Go ahead. Take a risk. It's O.K. to make a few intelligent mistakes. Try doing something new. Don't stop thinking, just stop playing it safe. So, you've made a few mistakes. So what. Learn from them and then forget about them. Mistakes ought to be springboards to the future.

The Cost of Tuition . . . After School

I remember when I purchased my first automobile. I was 17, a junior in high school, and I fell in love with it the moment I saw it. It was beautiful, a pale yellow, 1947 Studebaker coupe with a painted black top to make the car look like a convertible. With over 90,000 miles on the odometer and tires so worn the tread disappeared at the edges, it cost me all of a hundred and fifty bucks. Still, it was my car, my first car. Even the rust metastasizing around the wheels and under the headlights couldn't diminish the pure joy of ownership. This was a wonderful automobile, and it was mine. I couldn't wait to crank down its windows and take it for a spin.

I drove it all afternoon, around the neighborhood mostly, and then I decided to see what the thing would feel like on the highway. I headed north, out of town, where I could test the car on some serious asphalt. In a few miles, I found myself on State Highway 167, a more or less deserted rural road that curved back and forth across some of Wisconsin's most beautiful rolling farmland. The car swung into the curves and chewed up the straightaways like a dream. I settled back and let the miles go by. I hadn't gone more than 20 miles or so when I heard trouble. The engine coughed and sputtered. The power evaporated under my foot and, before I realized what had actually happened, the car had rolled to a quiet stop. I was out of gas.

I remembered passing a service station on the highway, about three miles back and, without a better idea of what to do, I started walking. Before long, the clouds thickened and it began to get dark. I was increasingly aware of how still it was. A few solitary cars passed at approximately 10-minute intervals, but none seemed willing to stop. Then it started to rain. Within minutes, the sky had blackened, the wind picked up and I was leaning into a torrential downpour.

It was 10:30 when I finally got home. Soaking wet from my three-mile hike, I was more than a little tired. As I sloshed into the house, my parents greeted me with a mixture of relief and anger. My mother seemed mostly relieved I was home but my dad harumphed and left the room in apparent disgust.

My grandfather, who lived with us at the time, had been sitting in the living room when I came in. But now, he moved to the kitchen where the action was. He loved a little excitement. He was from "the old country," he liked to say and though he spoke with a heavy accent and was never fluent in English, he loved to tell stories and quote parables. His favorites were the ones that taught lessons, the ones that enabled him to teach his grandchildren the truths of life. The thing I remember most was his ability to simplify, to capture the essence of a "lesson" in a crisp, tight little analogy that made it impossible to forget.

"What happened?" Grandpa asked.

"I was taking a drive in my car," I said. "I forgot to check the gas gauge."

He rephrased my answer in the form of a question almost as though he were setting the stage, "You ran out of gas and had to walk in the rain?"

"Yes, Grandpa," I replied, "I had to walk in the rain."

He looked at me with a mischievous grin and said, "Boy..." He always called me "boy" when he was about to share some tidbit of "old country" wisdom. "Remember this," he said. "Remember what happened today. There's a lesson here worth knowing."

"What's that, Grandpa?" I asked, not really wanting to hear what he was going to say.

Grandpa's eyes brightened. He leaned forward, capturing me in a steady gaze, and raised his index finger to emphasize the point, "If you don't use your head," he said, pausing to build suspense, "you gotta use your feet." I couldn't deny how right he was.

Unfortunately, I've had the occasion to remember that truth many times since that time I ran out of gas. "You've got to think, boy, if you want to have an easier life," my grandfather would say. "You've got to plan for problems to avoid them." What a lesson!

At 15, I had a job selling magazines from door to door. It was hard work—very hard work. I couldn't believe the number of doors on which I had to knock to get a sale. There must be some method, I thought, some technique which would help me score more often. I wanted to learn everything I could about selling, hoping I could improve my batting average, hoping I could make the job easier and get better results without so damn much work. I decided to put the problem before my grandfather.

He was delighted to hear about my interest in finding an easier path to success and riches in the world of door-to-door commerce. "Sit yourself down, boy," he said. "I want to tell you a story."

No surprise in that, I thought. "O.K., Grandpa, let's hear it."

The moment he started, I knew the story. I knew it by heart. I'd heard it dozens of times before and could see immediately how it related to my selling magazines. The story was about the "old country," back when my grandfather was a boy of 10. His father (my great-grandfather), a big man with a great red beard, made him chop wood for the stove. When Grandpa complained about the amount of work, my great grandfather articulated the lesson which is destined to be passed in our family from generation to generation like an heirloom.

He said, "Boy, if you wanna get chips . . . you gotta chop."

But the lesson I remember most, the lesson that is still appropriate today, still relevant in almost everything I do, was the one my grandfather taught when I was in my senior year in college. My family wasn't wealthy and I worked two part-time jobs to be able to pay the cost of tuition. I drove a taxicab week nights, and I worked the checkout booth at a downtown parking lot on weekends. Driving a cab was hectic but incredibly interesting and the time went by fast. The parking lot was different. It was quiet most evenings and I could study until 10 or 11 when the theaters let out.

One afternoon, I came home after school to grab something to eat before getting ready to leave for work. My grandfather was sitting in the living room watching me race around the kitchen. "Where you going?" he asked. I told him I was going to work.

"You're working a lot lately, aren't you?"

"I sure am," I said. "It's the cost of college tuition. It feels like we get an increase every semester. It's so expensive right now, I can't imagine what it will be a few years from now. Sometimes I wonder if it's worth it."

Then, my grandfather told me something I shall never forget. "Boy," he said, "the tuition they charge at that university of yours is peanuts. If you want to see how expensive tuition can be, wait 'til you get out here in the real world."

I never forgot that sage observation and to this day, whenever I make a mistake, I draw the number "one" in the air with my index finger as if to chalk one up for my grandfather. Then, if no one is listening, I sing, "Tuuu-ih-shunnnn!"

Persistence, Not Perfection

1964 is still vivid to me. It was my very first year in the medical equipment business. Our "warehouse," if one could call it that, was a 1,000-square-foot, split-level building which was built at the turn of the century for a plumbing company. By year's end, we had two employees—me, and another guy. My job was to sell franchised dealerships to pharmacists to help them get into the burgeoning home health care marketplace.

I spent the first four months binding manufacturer's tearsheets into a rudimentary catalog and outlining the features of our brand new franchise program which guaranteed an exclusive territory—one franchise per city. I also wrote and practiced a sales presentation. At last, I was ready. I packed a suitcase and washed the car. At 8:00 a.m. on Monday, I set off for what I hoped was going to be the first of many successful business trips.

My plan was to head north from Milwaukee to Fond du Lac, Wisconsin, about 50 miles away. I would call on a pharmacy, sell a franchise, and move on to the next city, Oshkosh, another 50 miles to the north. After selling a franchise in Oshkosh, I would continue north, selling franchises first in Appleton and then Green Bay, where I'd turn east to the port city of Manitowoc on the Lake Michigan coast. Of course, I'd sell a franchise in Manitowoc, and then head south to Sheboygan and Port Washington, selling franchises in each and completing a successful loop home. Seven cities, seven franchises—this was to be the spectacular beginning of a great career.

I arrived in Fond du Lac by 9:00 a.m. Monday morning, and took a driving tour of the city to get the lay of the land. I wanted to pick the single, best-looking pharmacy in town for our program. I stopped for coffee—several times; in fact, I took my time. Our program wouldn't go to just anybody, no sir! And, I admit it now, I was more than a little nervous.

The first pharmacist I visited gave me all of 15 minutes while he continued to fill prescriptions, and then, with startling abruptness, he showed me the door. I couldn't believe it. I had hardly gotten started. I barely mentioned our $1,500 franchise fee when he hustled me out of the place. "No problem," I thought. "Someone else will have our program."

It was noon by the time I finished Fond du Lac. I had seen every single pharmacy in town and not one was interested in our program. I couldn't believe it. I pushed on to Oshkosh, a half-hour to the north, and began calling on prospective franchisees. But by 5:00, I'd seen everyone. Nobody in Oshkosh wanted our program either. I was tired, worn out. I decided to drive to Appleton and check into a hotel. "Tomorrow," I told myself, "would be a better day."

I noticed signs on the highway for the Conway Hotel as I came into Appleton, and drove there directly. After checking into my room, I went down to the restaurant for dinner. The waitress seated me and asked if I'd like a drink. I ordered a martini, dry. I was never much of a drinker but there was something about this first day which seemed to require a dry martini.

As I sat there, nursing that drink, I realized what had happened. I was so inexperienced, so green, so wet behind the ears, I had actually *un*-sold every single person I talked to. I *un*-sold them! I'd seen every potential franchisee in two cities, Fond du Lac and Oshkosh, and I *un*-sold every one of them. And, in the process, I'd left a wake of destruction behind me unequaled since Attila the Hun swept through Europe in the 5th century.

"If this keeps up," I reasoned, "I'll be out of a job before we ever get this thing off the ground. Something's got to change. I've got to do something!" That's when I made what turned out to be a crucial decision. The next meeting, I would not see every single pharmacist in Appleton. I'd see *one*. Then, if I didn't sell that one pharmacist, I'd go on to the next city leaving some people behind, alive and breathing, so I could come back and talk to them later when, hopefully, I'd have figured out what I was doing wrong.

The next morning I dressed, had breakfast and set out to "do" Appleton. I scouted the south side of the city, found a decent-looking pharmacy and went inside to talk to the pharmacist. He was pleasant enough and gave me nearly an hour, but I *un*-sold him nevertheless. It took me all of 10 seconds to pack up my briefcase. I couldn't wait to get out of there. I thanked him for his time and walked back to my car. I got in, shut the door, and right then and there, I drew the number "one" in the air with my index finger and at the top of my lungs I screamed, "Tuuu-ih-shunnnn!"

I took a deep breath. It felt so good to scream like that inside my car with the windows shut. Building a business, I thought, was going to be much harder than I realized. I started the engine, pulled out of the parking lot and headed for Green Bay. I told myself I had the whole day ahead of me and I had a lot to learn. I had to figure out what these people wanted, what they needed which, obviously, our program wasn't providing. I had a lot to do.

When I arrived in Green Bay, I *un*-sold a pharmacist there and drove on to Manitowoc where I *un*-sold another one. Manitowoc was at the top of the loop, and now I'd turn south and head for home. On the way, I *un*-sold pharmacists in Sheboygan and Port Washington. In the ensuing months, I made other trips and *un*-sold pharmacists in Madison, Racine, Kenosha, Janesville, Beloit, Wausau, Stevens Point, LaCrosse, Eau Claire, Superior, Platteville—all over the state. It was awful. But I was learning and, at least, there were people I could go back to talk to.

Gradually, as I learned what was missing, I modified our program to meet the real needs of these pharmacies, not just the ones I thought they had. I reduced the entry fee from $1,500 to $500—$25 down and the rest over time and based on a percentage of the profits. After all, we had to get something on the map.

It still wasn't easy. I suffered setbacks and made mistakes. But, I was persistent. As my grandfather said, if you wanna get chips—you gotta chop.

By the time our business reached its sixth year, we were adding franchises at a decent clip and our entry fee had grown to $25,000. Two decades later, when we sold the company, we had franchises and dealerships in 385 cities in 45 states, from Maine to L.A. and from Anchorage to the Virgin Islands . . . and, listen to this: we still didn't have a store in Fond du Lac or Oshkosh.

Mistakes? Sure, I made 'em, but I was able to forget them. I believe that every recipe for success ought to call for a dash of amnesia. Forget your mistakes. After you've learned the lessons they teach, your mistakes can't do you any good.

Unfortunately, some people never seem to be able to let go of past mistakes. They hang on to the ones they've made, and process and reprocess the mistakes made by others. I never could understand it. It doesn't accomplish anything. It encumbers the freedom to take risks and gets in the way of doing new things. It is wasteful. It takes up energy which could be used accomplishing something for the future. When it's too late to go back and do things differently, what's the point of chewing on old errors? If a person makes the best decisions with information available at the time, so be it. Let it go. What's behind is behind. Look forward, not back.

Sometimes it's hard to see that you're making progress. When that happens, when you feel you're not getting anywhere, you can see that you've made progress when you look back at where you've been and remember where you've come from. The point is success is achieved in tiny parts, one day at a time. Work at being successful in bits and pieces and before you know it, you'll be accomplishing big, wonderful things. Years ago, I saw a cartoon which said it perfectly. Beneath the sketch of a man with a fork in one hand, a knife in the other and the improbable lump of an elephant on his plate read the caption: "The only way to eat an elephant is one bite at a time."

*   *   *

Summary

1. Don't make yourself so perfect in your present job that your boss will not see your value in a bigger job.

2. Don't limit yourself to things you're good at. Tackle something challenging. Take the risk of doing something new which you think will benefit your company.

3. Try to balance "Quality" with "Quantity." Sometimes you have to get the job done—not perfect—just done.

4. When you don't know something, be willing to say, "I don't know" and ask for clarification. Smart employees know that getting the facts is more important than projecting an image.

5. Be willing to make mistakes but avoid making foolish ones. Ignorance is correctable but stupidity can get you fired.

6. After you've learned from your mistakes, forget them. Look forward, not back.

7. Remember, success is achieved in bits and pieces. "The only way to eat an elephant is one bite at a time."

Chapter 5

The Ya-hoo Who Became
a Dynamo

"Imagination is more important than knowledge."
—*Albert Einstein*

In some ways, Dick Mathias and Jacob Jonas were very much alike. They started working for our company within one week of each other, and both started at an even eight dollars an hour. They liked their jobs, worked very hard and, of course, both wanted to get ahead. Yet, for a couple of very important reasons, their progress was not the same.

In the nearly 10 years Dick Mathias was with us, he was steady as a rock. First to come into the office in the morning and often the last to leave. Dick was a company man. He really cared about the organization and everyone knew it. He was intelligent, hard working and honest. Yet, Dick Mathias never got a significant promotion.

Underneath his manicured presentation and optimistic facade, Dick was a negativist. When we first decided to computerize our inventory, bookkeeping and billing systems, Dick warned against all the things that could go wrong. "If the computer goes down," he would say, "we'll never recover. We won't know what was shipped for three months. How will we ever get paid if we don't know what was shipped? And if we don't get paid, we'll lose money. And if we lose money, we won't get raises, or worse, we'll have to let people go." And on, and on, and on.

He had nothing good to say about data processing—or the people who worked there. "Those people just sit around all day and fix the

39

errors they made yesterday," he declared. "It's trial and error. Now they're talking about training meetings. Hell, I don't have enough hours in the day as it is."

Dick remained stuck in old patterns and clung doggedly to old habits. He was staid and stodgy, fixed in his routines. He hated change. His banner was "The tried and true"; his motto: "Don't mess with what is." In addition, he was extremely territorial; he regarded any suggestion from peers as meddling. He wanted no interference in his tiny kingdom. Dick Mathias was a stick-in-the-mud and, like many employees who resist change, he missed the best opportunities to get ahead.

Jacob Jonas, on the other hand, didn't seem like management material—not at first. He was a hardnose. When he thought he was right, almost no one could change his mind. The people who reported to him complained that he lacked understanding and compassion. They said he was rigid and stiff, and insisted he had no tolerance for human error. They said they didn't like working for him and several asked to be transferred to another department.

"Jake," as we called him, was willing to change. He knew he was not the kind of manager he wanted to be and decided he would find opportunities to learn. Every month or two, he asked for a meeting with me to discuss his department and his performance. He described problems he was having and let me know he wanted my input. He wanted to know how he could be more effective.

I advised him about his style with the people who reported to him and told him his communication with staff needed improvement. He took criticism well and was open to hearing that changes were needed. With practice, he became increasingly willing to adapt, willing to do what was necessary to become the kind of manager I wanted. He became flexible.

In addition to cultivating friendships with people at his level in the company, Jake made friendships with managers at higher levels. At work and in social situations, he kept his priorities clear. He came to meetings prepared, he came with ideas, and he came with solutions. He never engaged in inappropriate conversations about company problems and studiously avoided the company grapevine. Over time, Jake developed a manager's perspective. Knowing that all departments in an organization are interrelated and interdependent, Jake was interested in other managers' issues as well as his own. He became a team player.

Because of his ability to accept criticism and make changes, Jacob Jonas grew with the company. He seemed always ready to assume new responsibilities. "You bet! I'd love to handle that," was Jake's typical response to a new project. He never said things like, "Can't we get someone else to handle this, I'm already overloaded." Or "I just don't have the time."

Jacob Jonas always reacted to new responsibilities with an attitude that said, "I know that doing new things is the way our company can grow, and I want to help the company grow." Jake knew he could learn what he had to learn and grow with the job, even if he was a little scared of a new responsibility. It was clear he understood the company's growth and his personal growth were inextricably connected. What a great feeling it was to have someone willing, even anxious to take on additional responsibility.

Jake's Rules for Getting Things Done

There is a difference between people who always seem to be able to get things done and those who don't. Jacob Jonas had the technique down pat.

He would arrive each day full of energy. "Good morning, Good morning," he'd say as he passed the typing pool. "Hello. How are you?" he'd say as he hurried down the hall to his office. "It looks like a great day, doesn't it?"

He was like that every morning. He walked with purpose, saying hellos and good mornings while make a beeline straight for his desk. Sometimes, his energy was so focused, one couldn't be sure if he really knew anyone else was there. Jacob Jonas had things on his mind, tasks to handle.

After sliding behind his desk, he pulled a stack of papers from his briefcase and within minutes had an organized batch of work spread out in front of him. Apparently, he'd made a list of "things to do" and already had them prioritized. From his behavior each morning, it was certain he knew what he would tackle first. He knew it even before he got to the office. And, when he got to his desk, he wasted no time getting to it.

Often, he had gotten a good two or three hours' worth of work done before he even thought of having his first cup of coffee. Not everyone came in ready to go to work. It took some people an hour and a half just to get started. Others took a lot longer, like Dick, for example.

Dick was not at all like Jake. Before Dick started to really work in the morning, he'd have a cup of coffee, glance at the morning paper, straighten the top of his desk, visit the bathroom or kibitz with neighbors, all before getting serious about the work in front of him. People can waste time occupying themselves with trivia, and even minor work-related trivia just to avoid dealing with the important things requiring their attention. Procrastinators can be very inventive.

Jake was different. He knew how to get things done. He knew how to separate the productive from the wasteful. He had a routine, a system, a methodology which he practiced in the same way every day. He followed two simple rules, rules so productive he made them his dogma, rules so basic you'd think everyone would follow them.

First, among all of the many and varied things he wanted to accomplish each day, he selected the most important to do first, the one which would have the most impact on the company. Second, he wasted no time getting started.

This simple plan for prioritizing, tackling and finishing difficult tasks was so effective for Jake, he had his rules printed and framed. He even hung them on the wall in front of his desk where he could see them the first thing every morning. And, just to give them personality, to make them his own, he named them after himself. He called them: "Jake's Rules for Getting Things Done."

Jake's Rules for Getting Things Done

1. Rank things to do by their order of importance
   to the company.
2. Select the most important thing to do first
   and get started first thing in the morning.

In order to get started first thing in the morning, Jake couldn't take time to prioritize his work the first thing in the morning. That had to be done the day before. Sometimes he did his prioritizing at the end of the work day before he left the office, but more often than not he did it at home in the evening. By setting up his agenda before leaving the previous day or the night before, he was able to get to work in the morning knowing in advance what he was going to do.

Deciding what to do before you have to do it is the real key. It's like reading a road map before you get to the intersection. It's like knowing what you're going to say and taking the time to practice before walking to a podium to give a speech. That was Jake's methodology, his system. It gave him a head start, a momentum, an impetus to tackle big things and get them done.

We all will recognize parts of ourselves in this chapter. Whether there is a lot of "Jake" in you, or more of "Dick," can make a major difference in how effective you are in your own job. Obviously, if you are more like Jake than Dick, you are more likely to get ahead in your company—to get promoted. Reread Jake's Rules for Getting Things Done. And, maybe, you'll want to copy them and tack them up in front of you so you'll see them the first thing every day.

There were many things about Jacob Jonas that helped him become successful. Over time, I grew to trust him. I trusted his input and valued his straightforward thinking and businesslike perception. He never minced words or told me what he thought I'd like to hear. He told me what he saw, the way he saw it. Yet, I always knew I could count on him to represent our company in public to the company's best advantage even when he personally disagreed with a company position. Not surprisingly, Jacob Jonas's career flourished.

Bosses Promote People Who Think

Mary Ann McKinney, my long-time administrative assistant, was truly one of a kind. She started as a general secretary but, within a few months, she had made herself so valuable to me I made her my personal secretary. In the next year, she became my assistant and had supervisory responsibility for the rest of the secretarial staff.

Mary Ann's value had less to do with her skills and formal training than it did with a wonderful combination of perceptiveness, intuition and way of thinking. She had common sense. She understood something few other employees seemed willing to accept. She knew I wasn't perfect. Well, of course I wasn't perfect, far from it, and I had my share of criticism from employees to be sure. But, people seemed to expect perfection where I was concerned. Mary Ann didn't.

She knew my weaknesses and my strengths, and accepted them for what they were. She made my imperfections a part of the focus of her job. For example, she knew I loved the big projects and hated detail. She understood I was task oriented. Actually, I have tunnel vision in the straight ahead, single-minded way I tackle projects, and, when I'm in a tunnel, I'm very hard to reach. Mary Ann figured out how to work with me. She may not have liked it, but she made it her business to learn how to communicate with me.

To this day, I don't know how she could juggle a hundred unrelated matters all at the same time. I'm a one-thing-at-a-time person. So, she assumed responsibility for as much detail as she could and delivered the rest to me piecemeal. She never threw a bushel basket full of problems at me—she prioritized and tossed them one at a time. Instead of criticizing me for inattention to detail, she made the detail which plagued me part of her job. She relieved me of it so I could function in the way I do best. She helped me get the most out of every day. She wasn't afraid to give criticism either, when she thought it appropriate. But, always, it was given privately, with respect for my status and appreciation for my intentions.

Mary Ann was one hell of an employee. The essence of why she was so good can be summed up as follows: She accepted my inadequacies, made up for my deficits, and shaped her job to fit mine. She made my life smoother and easier. She made me better and more effective in my job. When you come right down to it, isn't that what all bosses want from the people who report to them? Isn't that what they want from every employee?

Mary Ann was able to make the transition from secretary to supervisor because she was willing to think. That may not sound like much, but it is. One of my pet peeves about employees who didn't think was the occasional vacant stare. It usually attacked when the employee had completed an assignment and was ready for a new project. And then came the question, "What would you like me to do now?" My problem was never with the question. It was that the next step was apparent if only the employee would think. I sometimes figured, if this person isn't interested in thinking, maybe he isn't interested in getting ahead.

If you want to get promoted, you have to be willing to think. Obvious, you say? Maybe not. It's easy to stop thinking. I know from my own experience. If I am working on something that doesn't interest me—let's say I'm helping my wife clean out the attic—I stop thinking with no effort at all. I give away my power and beg to be led. "What should I do now, honey?"

"Well," she answers, "you have torn up the empty boxes, so why don't you carry them to the trash?"

"O.K.," I respond listlessly and drag the boxes outside. And then, as I shuffle back from the trash bin, I yell, "Honey, what would you like me to do now?" It doesn't matter that the work is apparent. I'm not interested and so I'm not thinking.

If you want to get promoted, you have to be willing to think. We sometimes speak without thinking—as though we believe it doesn't matter what we say as long as we say something. I'm reminded of a story my father used to tell about the woman who went to the meat department in her neighborhood grocery store and asked the butcher the price of round steak per pound.

"Round steak, Madam," the butcher replied, "is $2.79 a pound."

"$2.79 a pound?" the woman exclaimed, "Why, that's robbery! At the butcher shop across the street, round steak is only $2.25 a pound."

"Then, Madam," the butcher said gently, "why don't you go to the butcher shop across the street?"

"I did," the woman answered quickly. "But, they don't have any."

The butcher looked at the ceiling in disbelief. Could she really mean what she was saying? If they were out of round steak across the street, what possible relevance could their prices have?

"My good Madam," he replied with experienced cool, "if we didn't have any round steak, ours would only be a buck-fifty a pound."

A New Way of Thinking

Moving into management requires a new modus operandi, a different way of behaving. It demands creativity, discipline and self-direction. Think about it. The lower you are on the rungs of the corporate ladder, the less these qualities are required of you and the more your supervisor juggles priorities and assigns tasks for you. You don't have to think. You don't have to make things happen. That's your supervisor's job. If Mary Ann McKinney had assumed this attitude with me, she'd still be in the secretarial pool.

As you move up, there is much less clarity about what you should be doing from moment to moment and more focus on organizational objectives. The higher up you go, the less structured the job—the more you have to be a self-starter. The challenge becomes less completing someone else's assignments and more creating assignments for yourself and those who report to you. There is pressure to find your own path, urgency to set your own goals and, when you are managing others, an expectation that you will get your team into shape and operating effectively. Doing this well requires new skills. It demands effectiveness in goal setting, creative planning and problem solving. And, it requires initiative.

When Keith Aspen started in our warehouse 20 years ago, he had the same job as a dozen other order pullers. He pushed an inventory cart through warehouse aisles and physically picked merchandise from shelves and filled orders. He packed boxes, loaded and unloaded freight trailers and restocked warehouse shelves, He came to us to work at the bottom of the totem pole, and, five years later, Keith was the warehouse manager.

Why? How did Keith move up? Keith was successful in part because he believed in himself, he had confidence in his abilities. Not only did he do his job extremely well, he saw himself as a thinking person. He thought beyond the assigned tasks and contemplated the process in which he was involved. He thought about how he might improve the system. He didn't simply accept things as they were just because they existed, he wondered how they could be better.

Within six months, Keith had developed a better method of product organization, designed a new series of printed signs which redirected order pullers through a more efficient route in the warehouse and created a staggered work schedule which virtually eliminated unnecessary overtime. Keith did not accept things as they were. He was always involved, always tuned in, always thinking, trying to improve the way we did things and often, though not always, succeeding.

Keith was flexible. He had a style, a way of behaving which made it easier for him to give what any boss wants. In a nutshell, he was committed. He wanted to deal with the broad picture, not just the job at hand. He had an ability to see beyond the day-to-day and focus on the future. In addition, Keith was a bulldog, he persevered, he didn't let the little things hold him back. To be a manager, one must have a sense of legitimacy, confidence in one's own ability, and believe that he or she can make a difference. Self confidence translates into the freedom to make changes. That's where Keith's power came from. How could I let a talent like that go to waste?

*   *   *

Summary

1. Ask your boss to make suggestions about your performance and how you could be of greater value to the company.
2. Be flexible, willing to change and adapt, willing to do what's necessary to become the kind of manager your boss wants.
3. Don't just work at accepting change, work at creating it.
4. Be willing to assume new responsibilities, and do so with enthusiasm and in a way that says, "I want to help the company grow."
5. Follow Jake's Rules for Getting Things Done: Prioritize, then attack the most important thing first thing in the morning.
6. Adapt your objectives to fit those of your boss and your company. Try to make your boss's life easier.

Chapter 6

Grapevines Grow Lemons

"Wise men talk because they have something to say; fools because they have to say something."

—*Plato*

Iwill never forget Will Callaghan. Every company has a grapevine, and Will Callaghan was the central figure in ours. If anything was happening—personal or professional—in anyone's life, Will would know what it was. He knew everything about everybody, from who was job hunting to who just got a promotion. He knew whose husband was sleeping with whom, how many drinks the personnel manager had the night before, who left dirty dishes in the lunchroom, how many breaks my secretary took each day. I even think he knew how many gold crowns I had on my back molars. No one was safe, nothing was sacred. Will was absolutely the best source of personal gossip in our company, bar none. Sometimes I wondered how he had time for his job.

"What's up, Will?" I'd ask.

"Did you hear about Charlie in shipping? He's having surgery on his foot next week. He's going to be asking for a couple of personal days, and then he'll be on crutches for two to three weeks."

I wondered if we knew that. One would think our personnel people would know about a planned surgery, but I couldn't be sure. It wasn't unusual to get new information from Will Callaghan. He frequently knew things long before I did. "Thanks for the dope on Charlie," I said.

"Think nothing of it," he replied with a broad smile. He just loved having information to share.

As I turned to head back to my office, he stopped me, "Wait a minute," he said. "I wanted to ask you where the Christmas party is going to be held this year."

Will was a trader. Information was his commodity and, whenever he gave some, he expected to get good information in return. "Gee, Will, I'm not sure yet," I replied. "As soon as I know, I promise you'll be the first."

"O.K. Boss," he responded in a cheery voice. "You know where you can find me."

I knew exactly where I could find him. The lunchroom was Will's hangout, his turf. To say Will Callaghan was connected inside our organization is like saying executives make more than the minimum wage. Will made it his personal business to touch base with as many employees as possible. I marveled at how he did it. He planned his breaks so they would coincide with those of others. He organized lunches and arranged after-work get-togethers. He never missed a party and gave a few of his own, all of which enabled him to maintain a constant, fresh supply of his commodity.

Will's connections crossed all lines. He had relationships with everyone from sales to accounting, from shipping to management. By anyone's standards, Will Callaghan's communication network was an intelligence-gathering masterpiece.

He shared tidbits of gossip with anyone who would listen. Fellow employees would gather around him glued to every word, relishing every morsel. Will must have felt pretty good with the constant attention his gossip generated. Even so, there never seemed to be enough.

My problem with Will Callaghan came down to one thing. I could never really trust him and I would never promote an employee I couldn't trust. If I had promoted him, how could I have been certain sensitive information would not find its way into the company's rumor mill?

Trust is the key. Trust is having confidence in another person. It is having faith in another's thinking and judgment, knowing in advance that his or her behavior will be appropriate in any circumstance. It is believing in the other person's integrity and ethics. It is being comfortable with another person in charge. It means being able to depend upon another person and being certain that difficult situations will be handled properly. It is knowing that responses to problems will be rational, prompt and effective. Having trust is having security.

Years ago, I had a conversation with the chairman of First Interstate Bank of Wisconsin. Our company had just started to borrow big money and I wanted to know what bankers wanted from their customers apart from the obvious—the timely payment of debt service.

He told me that bankers aren't really turned on by receiving loan payments. "We expect them," he said. "They're a matter of course in our business. We may be unhappy when they're not made on time, but interest payments do not in themselves provide much of a thrill for most bankers.

"There are," he continued, "two things that especially please bankers about their customers. One is when our customers have slightly larger balances in their accounts than we expect. The second is having no surprises."

"No surprises?" I said, not understanding fully what that meant.

"That's exactly right," he explained. "Bankers want to be able to trust their customers. They want to have confidence they really know what's going on. Bankers don't want to be surprised when bad things happen and, believe it or not, they don't want to be surprised when good things happen. Bankers don't want surprises, period. They want to know what's happening in their customers' businesses in advance because it gives them confidence their customers know what's happening. It's a matter of trust which requires honesty and competency, and mutual trust is what good banking relationships are all about."

All good business relationships require mutual trust just as good social relationships do, and trust is the one ingredient bosses must have in the employees they promote. Without trust, bosses won't share the most serious of their problems and, unless those problems are shared, the boss can't get help solving them. Bosses look to establish trusting relationships with their managers, and more often than not, when the employee is an active participant in the company grapevine, it eliminates the potential for doing so.

I don't deny the grapevine can be a useful tool for gaining insight into organizational and employee issues. Smart bosses understand this and tune in when they can. Bosses want to know what their employees are thinking and talking about, and grapevines can provide important clues. They want to know what problems may brewing so they can respond in ways that nip those problems in the bud. Employees, of course, are no different. They want to know about issues that may affect them. Having one's ear to the ground isn't a problem in itself—but when it affects your boss's perception of your trustworthiness, it is.

Will Callaghan's network of associations could have made him an asset. He could have become an opinion leader. His information pipeline could have served as a communication link inside our company, and every organization needs effective means for internal communication, both formal and informal. The problem was that Will didn't just gather information, he molded it, embellished it and passed it along to serve his own purposes. He used it to become information king.

Grapevines are mine fields, and maneuvering safely within them is difficult if not impossible. Had Will Callaghan been selective with the information he shared with others, he might have demonstrated the kind of judgment all bosses want in the people they promote. Instead, he demonstrated a lack of judgment which made him a serious confidentiality risk and virtually prevented him from getting promoted.

They Called Him "Animal"

We were in the last days of our company's move to new headquarters. We had been growing rapidly and desperately needed more room for warehousing and offices. I stood in our new reception area and looked across the room through the open doorway which led into the general office area. Then, I saw two of our managers shoulder to shoulder, walking backward across the doorway, carrying one end of a large, heavy desk.

Their faces showed the strain of the load as they backed out of view and, for a moment, the desk was all I could see through the doorway. As it jerked slowly past, I waited to see the people at the other end. Then I saw—him.

"C'mon, you turkeys, get the lead out!" he barked. A solitary, six-foot-six bear of a man, with arms as thick as my mid-section, effortlessly carried the other end of the desk. "You guys work for a living?" he shouted. "C'mon, dammit. Let's move it!"

I was introduced to him later that afternoon. Pizzas were ordered and about 40 people sat in the lunchroom eating and talking when Lynette Sanger appeared with the giant in tow. Lynette worked in shipping and, like many other employees, had enlisted family members and friends to help us with the move.

"I want you to meet my boyfriend," Lynette said, gesturing to the behemoth behind her. "We call him 'Animal.'"

"Hi, Animal, is that really what they call you?"

"Yeah, that's what they call me . . . If I let 'em," he snorted.

"Thanks for being here," I told him.

He put a huge arm around Lynette and said, "Think nuthin' of it. You got any beer?" Then, as if to punctuate his request, he belched one of the longest, loudest, window rattling burps I had ever heard.

"No, I'm sorry, we don't."

"Yup, I'd be surprised if you did." Then his eyes lit up. "By the way," he asked, "you need a truck driver or somethin'? I'm available if you need anybody. And, from what I see, you could use somebody like me. Your managers, the ones I've met, couldn't manage their way to the John."

My God, I thought, I'd have to be crazy to hire his guy. Why would I want someone whose attitude was so completely anti-establishment? After all, I am "establishment," and Heaven knows, what I don't want are employees antagonistic to management.

"No, not right now," I said. "Thanks though."

Your Associations Describe You

The truth was I would never consider hiring Animal. For the most part, our employees were supportive of one another; some even said our company was like having a second family. Animal just wouldn't have fit in.

He had no qualms about visiting Lynette during the day, which disrupted the work flow in her department. Sometimes I'd see him in the lunchroom talking loudly and using vulgar gestures. But, the biggest problem was his behavior at company sponsored social events. When he was at a company party, the outcome was predictable. He would have two or three drinks too many and become obnoxious. He'd tell loud, off-color stories to anyone within earshot. He'd even bellow his profanities across the room.

One morning, following a Christmas Party at which he was particularly disruptive, I called Lynette into my office. She seemed to know why she was there. "It's about last night, isn't it?" she said sheepishly.

"Yes, it is," I told her. "We have to set some new ground rules."

I tried to explain as gently as possible that her boyfriend's behavior at company get-togethers was no longer acceptable. I told her his inebriation was unacceptable and, unless he would abstain from drinking, he would no longer be welcome at those affairs. I also asked her to put an end to his frequent visits to the office and suggested she let him know that the employee lunchroom was intended for employees only.

The point of sharing this story has less to do with Animal and Lynette Sanger than it does with how an employee's associations impact the boss's perceptions and attitudes about the employee. Frankly, it's nobody's business with whom an employee chooses to associate, but we're all human and humans react to the things around them at emotional and subconscious levels. We're like juries who can't ignore devastating information about the defendant just because the judge instructs us to disregard it. Bosses do make judgments about their employees based upon their employee's behavior and the behavior of people with whom they associate. Fair or not, Animal had an impact on Lynette's prospects for promotion. The wise employee knows that subtle forms of judgment are always taking place. Whether or not opinions should be formed on the basis of one's associations is an entirely different issue. The fact remains they do.

Whom you choose to date or marry is nobody's business but yours. But when that person is disruptive at your place of work or at company sponsored social events, then, fair or not, your spouse or mate becomes part of your image, part of who you are and, accordingly, can hurt your chances for promotion. On the other hand, when your partner is well mannered and socially adept, he or she can strengthen your image, which enhances your ability to fit in. However inappropriate this may seem, the truth is persons with whom you associate can either diminish or improve your chances for promotion.

How Friendships Can Help You Get Promoted

Perhaps more to the point is that the relationships one chooses to make within the company can help. I can't overemphasize how important they are, or how neglected they are by employees from clerks to vice presidents. The relationships employees choose for themselves say a lot about their understanding of who is in power. They say a lot about who the employee is. They can enhance an employee's image, or they can work to diminish it.

Take Susan Blanchard. Hired fresh out of college, Susan was energetic, talented, proficient at her job and extremely likable. She wanted to get ahead, but she conducted herself like someone who didn't. Susan had an entry-level position that offered an eventual shot at a management spot, yet she chose to confine her relationships at work to people who couldn't help her get ahead. She developed loyalties with folks who were working at a job, not a career, which made it impossible for her to begin to think in positive ways about the company and her own opportunities for growth. She never cultivated relationships with superiors, so none knew much about her.

Certainly, one should make friends with people at one's level and below because these employees, too, have valuable insights to share. But, associations limited to fellow employees cannot broaden an employee's perspective, and they increase the risk of developing an attitude which puts management on one side and the employee on the other, and that won't win promotions.

The best strategy is to have a mix of friends—people at your level and people above. Regardless of the level, develop relationships with positive people—those who think well of the company, other employees and themselves. Avoid the negativists and complainers—they'll just diminish your own optimism. Cultivate friendships with people who can help you understand a management perspective, people who can relate to you from the employer's world.

One final word about friendships at work. Don't, under any circumstances, share your day-to-day gripes with friends at work. We all have gripes, but they should never be shared in casual social contact because they will come back to haunt you. I can't tell you how many times I heard what Julie told John at the bar last night. If you are unhappy with your company or your workload or your boss, tell your boss. Even tell your friends, but don't tell your colleagues at work.

*   *   *

Summary

1. Avoid participating in company grapevines knowing that, in the boss's view, they make you a possible confidentiality risk.
2. Choose the people with whom you associate knowing that, right or wrong, who they are says something about who you are.
3. If you have a problem at work, tell your boss—don't tell your friends at work.
4. Conduct yourself in ways that say to the boss you are worthy of the boss's trust.

Chapter 7

The Entitlement Trap

I find the great thing in this world is not so much where we stand,
as in what direction we are moving.

—Oliver Wendell Holmes

"Fer Chrissake," Ray Williams yelled. He had just walked into the
lunchroom and was speaking for the benefit of about 20 people on
their mid-morning break. "My landlord just raised the rent. My car
needs a transmission. My kid wants to go to college. How am I sup-
posed to keep up with it all?" He plunked into a chair across from the
soda machine and gave it a swift kick with the side of his foot. "Three
percent, with inflation the way it is that's what they gave me, a lousy
three percent!"

Ray Williams had just received a raise, and he wasn't happy about
it. Ray thought the company should have given him a bigger raise so
he at least could keep even with the rising cost of living. He kicked the
soda machine again as words alone weren't enough to express his frustration. "I just can't keep up," he repeated.

In point of fact, Ray Williams' wages had not been keeping pace
with inflation, and he was angry about it. He thought he was entitled to
regular cost-of-living increases. He thought it was his right. He
thought his employer wasn't being fair. He was angry because, without the kind of raise he wanted, he would have to suffer the pinch of
higher prices.

His anger was certainly understandable. I always felt compassion
for employees who were having trouble making ends meet. I've talked

with many other employers and I'm convinced most bosses feel the same. Bosses don't want people in their companies to suffer. But, at the same time, bosses are limited in what they can do by the requirements of their own jobs.

In the early years, when our company wasn't able to give cost-of-living raises, I wished our employees could know what I knew. While there was no way they could possibly appreciate what I was facing without my telling them, I still wished they could have seen how tight our operations had to be and how overextended we were at times. I wished they could have been with me at bank meetings where I tried to explain our company's long-term goals and provide comfort to single-minded loan officers. I wished they could have known how many sleepless nights and 18-hour days I had. Of course, they never could.

Ray Williams was not alone in his thinking. Many employees believed that rising prices in groceries, gasoline and other consumer goods is a problem employers should address. They believed the employer has a moral responsibility to keep employees' wages high enough to overcome the ravages of inflation.

Most employers do care about their employees' welfare and want their employees to do well, but bosses are burdened by an obligation they know must always come first. Bosses are responsible for the survival and prosperity of the enterprises they manage. Bosses know that if their organizations do not survive, none of their employees can survive. They know their organizations must do well before their employees can do well. They know that companies must prosper first in order for their employees to prosper later.

Obviously, there was a huge gap between my thinking and Ray Williams' thinking. In spite of the fact most employers do care about their employees' welfare, they know that cost-of-living increases have little to do with the company's immediate welfare. Right or wrong, unless they are part of a negotiated labor agreement, most employers are compelled to protect their organization's welfare first.

How to Bake a Bigger Pie

So, the question for employees is this: What is the surest way to get raises when they are not automatic?

It's easier for the employee to get a bigger piece of the pie when the employee's contribution increases the size of the pie. It's easier for a boss to give raises from new revenues than it is to give them by redistributing the current payroll. In other words, it's easier to be paid more if you're worth more. Therefore, the fastest and surest way to earn a raise is to find ways to increase the company's efficiency and productivity, to find ways to cut costs or increase sales.

Any contribution which has a positive impact on the company's bottom line will increase the employee's chances for a raise. The number of contributions possible may be as varied as the number of tasks performed in the organization. Receptionists can make every caller feel welcome. Customer service employees can work at improving customer satisfaction. Shipping department employees can reduce errors and increase efficiency. Transportation employees can improve transit time and decrease shipping damage. The list is endless.

Sales commissions are an excellent example of compensation directly related to productivity. Many top salespeople earn more than top executives, but most bosses are happy to pay large commissions because they are the direct result of new revenues.

If you want more money, don't list your needs for the boss. Rather, tell the boss how the company will benefit by giving you more money. Use an approach that is company- rather than employee-centered. Use an approach that says to the boss, "Look boss, of course I want to make more money. I know it, and you know it. I also know if you're going to spend more money, you want to get something in exchange." It's not a reward-me-for-what-I've-done approach. Rather, it is an approach that says, "Reward me for what I will do."

President John F. Kennedy said: "Ask not what your country can do for you. Ask what you can do for your country." Insert the word "organization" for "country" and you have my point.

Entitlement means: "I'm entitled to it, I've got it coming." This attitude is a steel trap for advancement-minded employees because it keeps them from thinking in positive ways about creating opportunities and doing things that will benefit the company. Cost-of-living raises may provide some comfort to employees who are not moving up, but the movers and shakers are looking for more. They want real challenges, real opportunities and real promotions with the potential for significant raises. These employees are not hampered by the inertia of entitlement. Hanging on to the belief that you are owed something simply because you are employed will not help you get promoted.

Sharing the Wealth

There are two truths about sharing the wealth:

1. EVERYONE WANTS A BIGGER PIECE OF THE PIE.

2. SHARING THE PIE IS EASIER WHEN THE PIE IS BIG THAN WHEN IT IS SMALL.

The problem with getting a bigger piece of the pie is, unless the pie gets bigger, getting a bigger piece necessarily means others in the organization will have to get smaller pieces. In an organization whose revenues are stagnant or declining, the boss must think long and hard about the impact of raises on the profitability of the firm.

Even in cases where profits are enough to support raises, there is still intense pressure on the boss not to give raises. The company's board of directors implicitly discourages payroll increases because raises diminish profits. And since there is nothing that demonstrates the boss's value to the company's directors more than growing profits, bosses are smart to have an eye on how to minimize payroll costs.

Every boss understands that growing profits are the best insurance with respect to his or her own job security. Though smart bosses know emphasis on growth in profit to the exclusion of growth in people will damage the company's long term potential, increasing profits are always a feather in the boss's cap. Raising the company's payroll rarely is. The employee, therefore, is not just in competition with other employees for payroll dollars—but with the company's bottom line too. Many employees have difficulty understanding this and accepting it as one of the facts of business life.

The message to employees who want to get ahead is clear. Stop thinking in the work-reward framework. Stop thinking from an entitlement position and begin asking yourself: "How can I handle more responsibility?" or "How can I contribute more to the company?" or more to the point:

WHAT CAN I DO TO HELP THE COMPANY BE MORE PROFITABLE?

The "Not-for-Profit" Myth

Sometimes, it felt dirty. I'd been working at producing it for more than two decades and yet, when I sat on the boards of some non-profit organizations, saying the word "profit" sometimes felt dirty. When I uttered the word inside the not-for-profit world, I found myself looking around to see if anyone within earshot was cringing.

Even in the private sector, a lot of employees think profit is a dirty word. I could sense an attitude on the part of some employees that making a profit was, somehow, immoral—as though it always involved the exploitation of others. For as long as I can remember, Hollywood movies and prime-time television programs rarely portray business and business people in a positive light. It sometimes feels as though our entire culture is inundated with anti-profit propaganda, and it always made me want to defend myself whenever I suggested that our company needed to make a profit.

The notion that profit is dirty may stem from the thinking that profit is the fruit of human exploitation. And, since even the word "exploitation" is bad in the minds of many, it follows that profit must be bad. At the bargaining table, some labor unions still press the point that, because profit results from the efforts of employees, the bulk of it should be distributed to them and not retained in the company.

If plant and office equipment didn't wear out and need replacement or repair, and if markets didn't change, there might be no need to retain profits in the company. But that is not reality. Both for-profit companies and their not-for-profit counterparts must repair and replace old equipment. To stay viable, they must study the changing marketplace and invest in research and development. They have to create new products and new services to meet always changing consumer demand. Profits must be reinvested in order to grow or, at the very least, to maintain future market share.

"Future," that's the key word. "Profit" is merely the synonym. It is the fuel that drives the engines of innovation. It is the means and motivation for creativity and productivity, and it enables employees with energy, ideas and focus to grow and prosper. Profit is the grease of prosperity—the company's and the employee's. Nothing encourages the boss to give raises or promotions more than the perception that the employee will contribute to the company's ability to make a profit. If you want to get ahead, therefore, stop thinking that the company's profits justify a raise and start thinking about how you can earn a raise by increasing the company's prosperity.

What about those employees who work in organizations identifying themselves as "not-for-profit?" Are they, in fact, not concerned with profit? Is it true that profit does not motivate the behavior of their executives and employees? While the nation's many non-profit organizations and the wonderful people who work for them contribute significantly to the public good, I don't believe they are driven purely by altruism. Not-for-profit organizations struggle with the identical issues that dominate the thinking in their for-profit counterparts. Like any business, they must generate revenues to cover today's operating costs and pay for tomorrow's growth.

Their executives and employees want raises and promotions like everyone else. It may be true that some individuals who work in non-profit organizations think of themselves as cleaner and purer because they are free of the dreaded profit motive. Yet they, like their private-sector counterparts, want very much to prosper personally. And, of course, there's nothing wrong with that.

The notion that morality and purity of purpose is intrinsic to the not-for-profit endeavor is a myth. Whether it's called "profit" as it is in the private sector, or euphemistically referred to as "surplus" as it is in the non-profit arena, it is the same. Every organization wants it and the health of any enterprise depends upon it. In either environment, for-profit or not-for-profit, apart from differences in constituencies and the process by which resources are distributed, the dominant management imperatives remain the same: Provide a quality product or service, increase revenues and minimize costs. Success in any organization is calculated by the same arithmetic, and profit is the measure of the difference.

* * *

Summary

1. Let go of all "I've got it coming" positions and ask instead, "What can I do to help the company cut costs, improve efficiency and increase sales?"

2. Ask not what your company can do for you. Ask what you can do for your company.

3. Nothing encourages the boss to give raises or promotions more than the perception that the employee will contribute to the company's ability to make a profit. If you want to make more money, help the company make more money.

4. Understand that "profit" is not a dirty word. "Profit" means "future." It enables companies to repair and replace old equipment, to invest in research and development, and to grant raises and promotions.

5. The "not for profit" label is a misnomer. Whether it's called "profit" or "surplus," every organization needs it. Success in any organization is achieved by increasing revenues and minimizing expenses.

Chapter 8

How to Think Like a Boss

Thinking is the hardest work there is, which is the probable reason why so few engage in it.

—Henry Ford

A few days after our first meeting, Harry Porter was back for more. Standing in the doorway to my office, he asked, "Are you ready?"

"Sure, Harry," I said. "Come on in."

He came into the room and sat down in the chair in front of my desk. "I've been looking forward to this all week," he began. "You've given me a lot to think about, but what I really want to get from you are specifics about what I have to do to get ahead."

I looked across my desk at him. "Harry, the reason I promote some people and not others is really very simple and, if you understand it, you will know exactly what you have to do to get ahead."

Harry moved forward in his chair. "I'm all ears. This is what I want from you."

"O.K. Harry," I said. "No holds barred. Here it is. If you want a future in this company, you've got to stop looking out for your needs, and begin taking care of mine."

Harry's mouth fell open.

I went on, "In short, Harry, I give people promotions when I think they can help me do a better job. I promote people when I think they can handle more responsibility and help me get things done in the process. I promote people when I think they can take some of the load off my shoulders. What it comes down to is this, Harry. I help people get ahead when I think they can help me get ahead.

"And frankly, Harry," I added, "I'd love to promote you, because I need as much help as I can get. But first, you need to change your thinking. You have to stop looking at things the way you have been and begin to see things the way I do because that is the only way I'll feel comfortable sharing responsibility with you. It boils down to this: I want people with an executive perspective, people who think the way a boss thinks."

Harry looked at me quizzically. He had been wondering about who was responsible for his not getting ahead and now he saw the possibility it might have been my fault. "Shouldn't you have been telling me this from the beginning?" he asked.

"Yes, I should have," I said. "You're right, I should have told you this long ago. If I had, I could have helped you and I certainly could have helped myself. If I'd told you earlier how to get ahead, why I promote people, you could have started doing the right things from the start."

"Right. You never told me any of this," Harry complained. "I've just been doing what I thought you wanted. If you wanted me to do things differently or think in a different way, you should have told me."

"Hold on a minute," I said. "I'm not denying my own responsibility here, but you can't use my failures as an excuse for not taking care of yourself. What if we hadn't had this conversation? There are hundreds of employees in this company and, as much as I'd like to sit down and talk to each and every one of them, just as I'm talking to you, that just isn't practical. That means it's up to you to take the first step."

The Key to Personal Power

"It's about personal power, Harry. You need your own power. You can't afford to sit around and wait for someone to come along and grant your wishes and make your life better. If you give your power away by making me the reason you haven't done all the right things, it leaves you weak and helpless. You've got to have your own power, Harry. Bosses don't promote powerless, helpless people.

"It comes down to initiative. It's a 'take charge' attitude, a readiness to take ownership of a problem. People who assume responsibility for themselves and the things around them have a certain kind of power. It's like charisma—it surrounds them. Kids know their parents have it. Employees know their bosses have it. And, Harry, for your own sake, you've got to have it too. I can't promote you without it.

"The willingness to get into action and take responsibility, to take ownership, is the way bosses think—the way they have to think. Don't you see, Harry? It's 'Boss Think,' and that's what I look for in all the people I promote."

How Much Is a Pack of Chewing Gum?

"There are two kinds of thinking, two universes," I said. "One is a boss's universe; the other is an employee universe. Unfortunately, too many employees confine their thinking only to themselves and the immediate tasks in front of them—that's too small a universe. A boss, on the other hand, must think about issues which affect the whole department or, in some cases, the entire enterprise. This kind of thinking is different, it's broader.

"Let me give you an example of this broader perspective. Several months ago, a 15-year-old kid was caught shoplifting in one of our pharmacies. A clerk spotted the kid pocketing a package of chewing gum and confronted him at the exit. During the brief commotion that followed, the kid repeatedly denied he had stolen anything. Finally, when it was clear no one was buying his story, the kid asked, 'Why are you making such a big deal out of a lousy pack of gum? It's only worth about 40 cents,' he argued. 'After all, this place can certainly afford a few dimes. Can't it?'"

Harry had no trouble understanding that our company took shoplifting very seriously. We had talked about the issue in numerous staff meetings and posted numerous reminders so employees would stay on their toes. But, when faced with so small a theft as a 40-cent pack of gum, I could tell Harry wasn't sure what the wider issues were.

"What are you thinking, Harry?" I asked.

"Well," he replied, "I don't see why we should care so much about the theft of one pack of chewing gum."

"Tell me, Harry," I said. "What is the cost to our business of one stolen 40-cent package of chewing gum?"

"I'm not sure," he responded. "I suppose it's 40 cents." He thought a moment. "Maybe it's less. The cost of the theft is probably only the wholesale cost of the package of gum. You know," he continued, "what we paid for it."

"That's correct," I said, "but let's take it a step further. At the end of the year, after we deduct expenses from our total revenues, what do you call what we have left?"

"Our profit," Harry quickly replied.

"Right. And do you know that, on average, pharmacies and grocery stores in this country make a net profit of about five percent or less?"

"No, I didn't. I thought they made about 40 or 50 percent."

"A lot of people think businesses make 50 percent in profit or more," I reminded him. "We may have a gross profit of between 40 and 50 percent—our sales minus the cost of the merchandise we sell— but it's easy to forget the cost of running a business, things like heat and electricity. And there are other costs such as telephone expense, supplies, advertising, insurance, interest on our business loans, and, of course, our biggie—payroll. Most retail operations in the United States are delighted if their net profit is anything close to 10 percent. We are averaging about five percent."

"I didn't know that," he admitted.

"So, if the net profit in our stores averages about five percent, isn't it fair to say our profit on a pack of gum is also about five percent? The other 95 percent," I said, "covers the wholesale cost of the gum—what we pay for it—plus the costs of running the business.

"Here's the crux of the issue. When a pack of gum is stolen, the question for the owner of a business is: How many packs do we have to sell to recover the cost of the theft? Since the profit on a pack of gum is five percent of the sale, or about two cents on a 40-cent pack of gum, each sale can only contribute those two pennies of profit to the recovery of the theft."

"Hold it," he said, "I've got it. You're saying, if someone steals a pack of gum, we have to sell more than one pack of gum to recover the cost of the stolen pack."

"You've got it, Harry," I came back. "We have to sell 19 packs to get back to even."

"Just think about what it costs us when someone walks away with a radio or a camera or something expensive like that," Harry declared.

"You don't know how good it feels to hear someone else say that," I said. "But don't stop there, Harry, because the cost of that stolen pack of gum is even more."

"How?" he asked.

"Well, since there is a limit to the number of gum buying customers any one store has," I said, "when we sell 19 packs of gum to recover the cost of a stolen pack, we also lose the net profit we would have earned from those 19 sales. That's profit that goes into the stolen pack of gum. It doesn't go into our cash register."

"That is really something," he admitted. "I don't think most people see it that way. I never did."

Harry Porter had now begun to think in the employer universe. He had begun to see the employer's reality. Understanding the real cost of shoplifting is just one example where employees often fail to see things as their bosses have to see them.

Seeing the Employer Universe

I remember an enthusiastic suggestion made by one of our top sales people a few years back. She wanted the company to outfit our sales team in brand new automobiles because she thought it would help build morale and raise the energy level of our sales force. She was correct, of course, about the impact the new cars would have had on morale. After all, anyone would like a new car. But where in that suggestion was consideration given for the rest of the company? What thought was there to the cost of implementing the suggestion? What analysis was made as to any negative impact it might have had on employees in other departments?

One of the mistakes employees sometimes make is assuming there is always a ready pool of cash in their company. One can hear it in what they sometimes say: "The company can afford it." "Just put it on the expense account." "They will probably just write it off." All of these suggest those employees believe the company can spend any amount of money without impact. "Boss think" recognizes the company's money has to be managed carefully. It understands that everything from a new piece of equipment to an extra paid sick day has a price tag attached.

"And so, Harry, that brings me back to the beginning. Bosses have to think about the entire organization, how all the pieces fit together. Employees who know this, who see the big picture, who can focus on the company's goals and understand that everything from shoplifting to free coffee has a price tag attached to it are seeing the world the way the boss has to see it. They have less trouble understanding that the company has limited financial resources and spending on one thing diminishes the company's ability to spend money in another area.

"These are the employees, Harry, who think like a boss. These are the ones who understand that every decision must be viewed in a context, as a part of the whole. Bosses are comfortable sharing responsibility with employees who see things this way, and these are the employees they promote."

I looked at my watch and realized, if I didn't leave soon, I'd miss an important meeting. "I've got to call time, Harry," I said. "I'll be late for a meeting if I don't leave here within the next 10 minutes. What do you say, can we pick this up again tomorrow at, say 5:30?"

"Sure thing, same time, same place."

"Right here tomorrow then."

I started to get up when Harry interrupted. "Hold it a minute. I just want to tell you how much I appreciate the time you're giving me."

"The feeling is mutual, Harry. You've made me realize I should be having these talks with more people. It's made me stop and think. You and I might never have started talking if you hadn't come in here. You're to be congratulated for initiative, Harry."

"Thank you," he said. "Now you better get going or you'll be late for your meeting."

"Right," I responded. "Thanks, Harry. I'll see you tomorrow, then?"

"You bet," Harry answered. "Tomorrow."

*   *   *

Summary

1. Bosses want to feel comfortable with the people they promote, and in order for them to do that, employees have to share their boss's perceptions of the company's problems.

2. Bosses look for a "take charge" attitude, a readiness to take ownership of a problem.

3. "Boss Think" is recognizing that everything has a price tag and knowing that part of the profits have to be put back into the company.

4. Think about the company's money as though it were going to come out of your own pocket.

5. People who assume responsibility for themselves and things around them have an aura of power bosses value.

Chapter 9

The Benefit of Being Understaffed

He who wishes to secure the good of others has already secured his own.

—Confucius

I'll bet there isn't a boss anywhere, at any level, who hasn't heard these words from an employee: "What we need in this department is more people!"

Gus McCann, one of the brightest of our maintenance department technicians, now had me captured in our lunchroom. "There's too much to do and we can't possibly get it all done because we're just plain understaffed."

"O.K., Gus," I said. "Maybe we can sit down and talk about it."

"What's there to talk about?" he asked. "We're not going to add people anyway. We never do."

If any issue separates the employer's universe from the employee's, this one does. The natural tendency of employers to want to limit the number of employees in order to keep payroll costs down runs headlong into the natural and understandable desire of employees to avoid the stress of too much work.

It was always one of the most frustrating issues for me personally because I found it so difficult to explain my point of view in a way that seemed satisfactory to most employees. Perhaps I was too close to the situation. Now, with the benefit of hindsight, let me try.

Think of an organization's workforce as a number of people, each with 40 hours of available time per week to spend on work. In other words, think of the workforce as an inventory of labor hours. In this sense, the number of labor hours a company has available to do work is directly related to the number of people employed. So, if a company has one person on the payroll, it has an inventory of 40 labor hours per week. If it has two people, there is an inventory of 80 labor hours per week, and so on.

In most departments, the workload (the demand for labor hours) varies from week to week. (See figure 1.) Since the workload fluctuates and is never constant, if an organization has enough employees when the workload is highest, it will necessarily have too many people at those times when the workload diminishes.

From a boss's point of view, the optimum number of employees in an organization is the number of employees who can get the work done over the long term. For this reason, bosses tend to employ only enough people to handle the average workload. Bosses understand there will always be times when their employees cannot get all the work done, but they also know there will be times when there isn't enough for everyone to do. (See figure 2.)

Bosses understand that the way to keep payroll costs in line over the long term is to allow the workload to get too heavy now and then. The solution, they know, is to have their employees handle the excess work during easier periods.

In the ideal circumstance, employees anticipate future work and do it in advance during periods when the workload is relatively light. When this isn't possible, overtime hours may be necessary—though overtime is always extremely costly. Another solution when workloads are heavy is to set priorities and do only the most important work, putting that which is less important aside for a later period when the workload has lightened.

Employees who understand this will accept as normal and natural the times when there are more things to do than there are people to do them. They will appreciate that a properly staffed organization will always have periods when it is understaffed. They will understand that those periods occur in all organizations and, because they understand that, will tolerate them with good humor.

Unfortunately, Gus McCann's resentment of an occasionally heavy workload is typical of many employees. He had stopped thinking and started believing, "It's always like this." Call it anger, call it burnout—

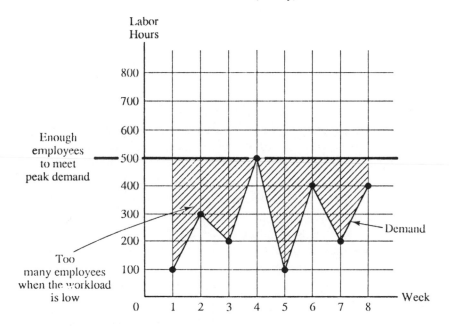

WORKLOAD
Demand for Labor Hours
(weekly)

Figure 1. Since the workload or demand for labor hours is never constant, if an organization has enough employees when the workload is highest, it will have too many people at those times when the workload diminishes.

it doesn't really matter. Whatever you call it, it's counter-productive. Employees who understand that it's normal for workloads to vary will impress their bosses with their ability to think in broad terms and in so doing will enhance their chances for promotion.

The boss wants managers who understand that getting the job done with the fewest number of employees costs less and is, therefore, in the company's interest. They also understand that, if the company prospers, they too will have the opportunity to prosper. The boss wants managers who understand this reality, who understand that not having enough employees all of the time is not only normal—it's desirable. That is the boss's reality. Except on an assembly line, and some-

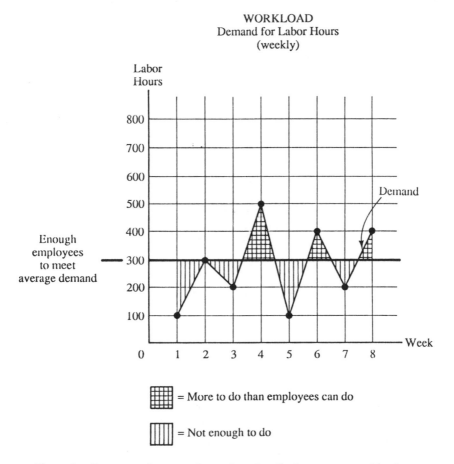

Figure 2.   Bosses employ enough people to handle the average workload understanding there will always be times when their employees cannot get all the work done. They also know there will be times when there isn't enough for everyone to do.

times there too, not having enough employees *all of the time* is desirable!

Employees who want to get promoted must understand the company's need to control costs. They must appreciate that one of the most effective ways to control costs in any organization is to manage its personnel costs. Another is to manage inventory.

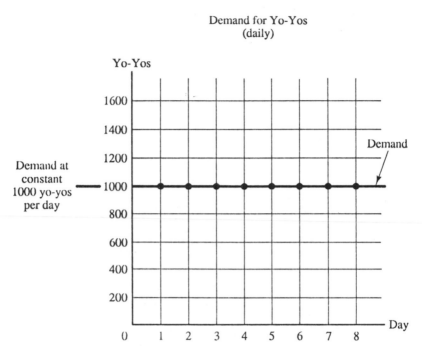

Figure 3.   If the demand for yo-yos is a constant 1,000 per day, there is no need to stock more than 1,000 yo-yos at any time.

When Enough Inventory Is Too Much Inventory

For purposes of illustration, let's examine the XYZ company. Assume that XYZ company manufactures yo-yos. After the yo-yos come off the assembly line, they are packaged and put on the company's warehouse shelves to await shipment to customers. Also assume the company has an unlimited manufacturing capacity and can make as many yo-yos every day as it needs.

Finally, let's assume the demand for XYZ yo-yos (the number of yo-yos the company sells) is a constant 1,000 yo-yos per day. Customers buy 1,000 yo-yos every day—never more, never less. The question for this illustration is : What's the minimum number of yo-yos XYZ company should stock for shipment each day?

If the demand for yo-yos is a constant 1,000 per day, there is no

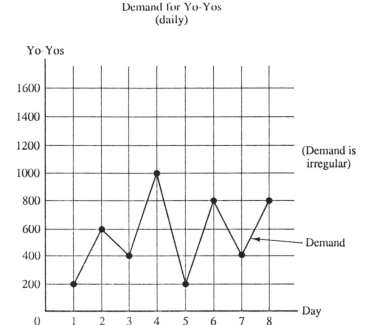

Figure 4.   In the real world, demand for a product or service is
never constant.

need to stock more than 1,000 yo-yos at any time. After all, the XYZ
company has no reason to make more than it needs for sale because the
more yo-yos it has on the shelf, the more money it will have tied up in
inventory. And, if money is tied up in inventory, it can't be available
for other things. (See figure 3.)

When demand is constant, it is predictable, and determining how
much inventory to stock is relatively easy. In the real world, however,
demand for a product (or service) is never constant. Today, the XYZ
company may sell 1,000 yo-yos, and the next day it may sell none.
The day after that, the company may sell 2,000 yo-yos, and so it goes,
because in the real world demand is never constant. (See figure 4.)

So let's ask the question again: When demand fluctuates from day to
day, what's the minimum number of yo-yos XYZ company should
stock for shipment each day?

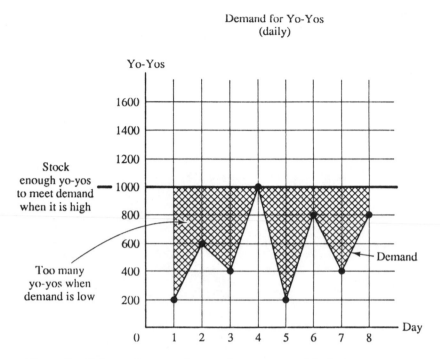

Figure 5. If the company stocks enough yo-yos to satisfy its customers on days when demand is high, it will have too many yo-yos on days when demand is low.

If the company stocks enough yo-yos to satisfy its customers on days when demand is high, it will have too many yo-yos on days when demand is low. (See figure 5.) On the other hand, if the company stocks only enough to satisfy its customers on days when demand is low, there will be other days when the company cannot meet customer demand for yo-yos. And every boss knows that when a company cannot meet customer demand, it will have unhappy customers. Having unhappy customers may mean losing sales today. But worse, if unhappy customers choose not to come back, it will mean losing sales in the future, and that's not good for business. (See figure 6.)

While low inventories and happy customers are goals of every business, they are sometimes contradictory, even mutually exclusive, goals. The challenge is to find the appropriate balance between low

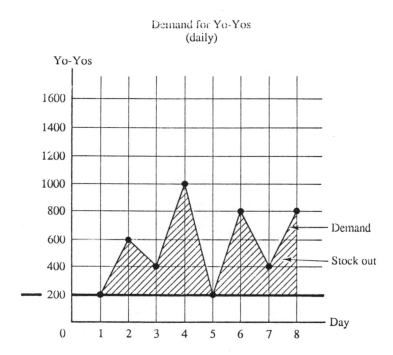

Figure 6. If the company stocks only enough to satisfy its customers on days when demand is low, there will be days when the company cannot meet customer demand.

inventories and happy customers. (See figure 7.) Employees who understand this problem are likely to be helpful in solving it. And, employees who help solve the company's problems are the most likely to get promoted. It is part of what bosses want from the people they promote.

How to Think Like an Investor

Since bosses represent the interests of investors in the enterprise and manage resources on behalf of those investors, the better bosses make it their business to understand what their investors want. And so it is useful for employees who want to become managers to also understand what investors want. The key to that understanding is to learn to think like an investor.

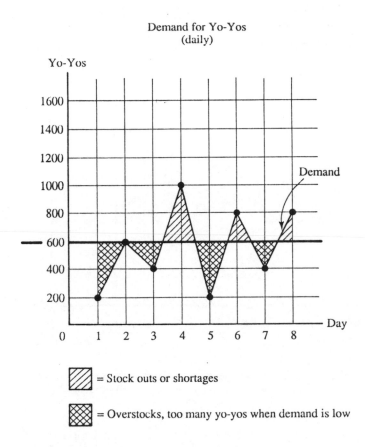

Figure 7.   Low inventories and satisfied customers are often mutually exclusive goals. Since both are costly, the challenge is to find the appropriate balance. If it were possible to measure accurately, the ideal balance is where the cost of excess inventory equals the cost of unhappy customers.

Let's use a simple example. Assume you have $10,000 to invest and have identified the following investment options:

A. A savings account paying 5 percent per annum, which means your $10,000 investment will earn $500 in interest in one year.

B. A 1-year bank certificate of deposit paying 7.5 percent, which means your $10,000 investment will earn $750 in interest in one year.

C. A business that could be purchased for $10,000 and that produces a net profit of $1,000 per year, which means the rate of return on your investment (R.O.I.) would be 10 percent in one year.

Assuming there is equal risk in all three investment opportunities, you would have good reason to buy the business because you would get 10 percent R.O.I., or the highest rate of return on your investment.

From an investor's point of view, the profit a business makes must be at least equal to the rate of return his investment can earn in a savings account or certificate of deposit. Otherwise, he would be better off liquidating his interest in the business and putting his money in the bank. For this reason, bosses know their businesses must make a profit at least equal to interest paid on savings instruments to keep their investors happy.

Every company in the private sector has investors. They are the owners of the business. A company can have thousands of investors as do most publicly held companies, or as few as a single investor as in the case of a sole proprietorship. Whether few or many, owners of a business, like all investors, want to get the highest rate of return possible on their investment.

Let's adjust the example. Suppose you wanted to buy the business described above, but were able to negotiate a better price than $10,000—let's say $5,000. In this case, assuming the business continues to produce $1,000 per year in net profit, the rate of return on your investment would increase from 10 percent to 20 percent, because your investment would be cut in half.

From an investor's standpoint, therefore, owning a profitable business depends not only on how much profit the business makes, but also on the amount of investment the owners have in the business. All other things being equal, the lower the owners' investment in the business, the more profitable their investment is likely to be.

And that brings us back to the need to control costs in general, and staffing in particular. Part of the reason Gus McCann was under so much stress when the workload was heavy was that Gus wanted "enough" time to produce the highest quality possible. I appreciated the fact that Gus took pride in his work, but I realized it didn't come without some cost to the company. What the company needed was someone who took the minimum time to produce a quality product.

Though conscientious, Gus was always slow and exceedingly deliberate. When we weren't busy, Gus did just fine. But when the pace picked up, Gus had trouble keeping up and, underneath it all, he didn't want anyone else to keep up either. So, whenever the workload increased, Gus sounded his usual alarm: "We're understaffed. We need more people. There's only so much a body can do and still keep the quality up."

Gus McCann was a product of the *Be Good—Get Reward* belief system, and like many employees, he measured his value to the company in terms of the quality of his output. Quality, of course, is important to every company. No boss will argue for poor quality, but quality at any price is not desirable.

I used to tell my managers we could do any job to perfection if we had unlimited time and enough people on the payroll. Getting a job done well is, in itself, no accomplishment. The accomplishment is in getting a job done well at the lowest possible cost.

*   *   *

Summary

1. Know that there will always be times when employees cannot get all the work done. There will also be times when there isn't enough for everyone to do.
2. Accept the fact that a properly staffed organization will have periods when it is understaffed and learn to tolerate those periods with good humor.
3. Understand that getting the job done with the fewest possible number of employees is in the company's interest.
4. The profit a business makes must be at least equal to the rate of return the owners of the business could earn in a savings account or certificate of deposit.
5. Understand that, if your company prospers, you too will have the opportunity to prosper.

Chapter 10

When to Violate a Company Policy

We need to add to the three R's, namely Reading, 'Riting and 'Rithmetic, a fourth—Responsibility.

—*Herbert Hoover*

Understanding what your boss really wants is critical to one's advancement potential. Unfortunately, employees sometimes make assumptions about what is wanted and miss the target, hurting their chances for promotion. Perhaps more to the point, a distorted view of the boss's reality can not only eliminate the prospects for promotion, it can trap you in your current job or even lead to termination.

Richie Green is a good example . We hired Richie to run one of our retail stores. He came to us with wonderful credentials, glowing references and a documented history of success in sales. I was excited about him and thought he would fit in beautifully. What I didn't know about Richie Green was that his definition of performance excellence was: "Work hard, make as few mistakes as possible, and do what you are told." No question about it, Richie knew how to follow orders. He could be counted on to follow directions exactly. Who would guess that such a meticulous strategy would get Richie into trouble?

As is common in many retail businesses, we experienced occasional difficulty with bad checks. In an effort to get the situation under control, we developed a policy requiring store clerks to verify customers' identification by writing their driver's license numbers on the back of their checks.

Richie's management problems surfaced when a customer presented a check and was unable to produce a driver's license. The customer was an older woman who had not driven an automobile in several years and saw no reason to have a driver's license. She offered her social security card and two department store credit cards as a substitute means of identification. Following our policy, the store clerk refused to accept the customer's check without a valid driver's license. The customer asked to speak to the store manager and Richie Green was called over to handle the problem.

She explained to Richie that she no longer drove a car and had, therefore, no need to carry a driver's license. Again she offered the credit cards and suggested they ought to be more than adequate for identification, but Richie was not convinced. He had memorized our store policy and was prepared to enforce it to the letter. "I'm sorry, Ma'am," he said politely. "We have a store policy here that says we can only take a personal check if we see a valid driver's license."

The customer left the store embarrassed, frustrated and angry. Richie, on the other hand, grew increasingly self-righteous and critical of the customer for not understanding that "Every store has policies." He even called the clerks together to reemphasize the need to maintain company policy.

The unhappy customer wrote me a long letter, and I followed up with a phone call. She did not mince words. "You should know, in all the years I've shopped at your store no one has ever treated me that way. Those people," she said, referring to our clerk and Richie Green, "treated me as though I were some kind of vagrant just because I didn't have a driver's license. I want you to know." she emphasized, "I will never come back to your store again. Never!"

The Real Goal: Creating Happy Customers

I immediately arranged a meeting with Richie Green. I told him I expected all of our employees—especially our store manages—to be able to think on their feet. I explained that, while our policy of verifying a customer's identification for personal checks was necessary, one of our most important goals was to create happy customers. That, I explained, is the only way to build business. A store manager must be prepared to overrule any single store policy when it becomes clear that it is counter-productive to the company's main goals.

"Richie," I said, "given the situation, you should have overruled our driver's license policy in order to keep this customer happy. No matter how carefully an organization's policies are developed, there will always be times when they don't serve the company's long-term goals. Your job as a manager," I told him, "is to sort through the issues when a problem arises, and then make some intelligent decisions.

"That's the reason we have managers. Most people can follow directions if the directions are clear enough. We have managers so we'll have someone around to think, someone who can identify a conflict between our policies and our goals, and then take action to resolve it. That's the manager's role. We can't run our business on automatic pilot. We have managers so we'll always have someone around who is willing and able to think."

This was beyond Richie Green. "I was just following orders," he said defensively. "If the policy was wrong, don't blame me."

Richie missed the point. He couldn't see the problem from my point of view. He couldn't see beyond our written policy and understand that businesses exist to serve people today, tomorrow, and the days and months after that. Those are the long-term goals. A business can survive and prosper only if it implements its policies in a way which helps it reach those long-term goals. Richie never got to the place where he could see this point of view and, eventually, we had no choice but to replace him with someone who could.

There are many situations in which employees don't see things in the same way their bosses do and that's a big problem for both the boss and the employee. I'm not saying everyone must agree with the boss's point of view, or even like the boss's point of view. But, if you want to get ahead in your organization, then you must understand your boss's viewpoint and operate accordingly. How else can you perform as he or she wants?

Thinking is the foundation for understanding what is expected of you. It's never enough to understand the literal meaning of directions given to you, you must also understand the intent. You must be in tune with the purpose of the directive and comprehend what your boss wants to accomplish in order to fully appreciate what is expected of you.

My grandfather loved to talk about rural Europe at the end of the 19th century. In those days, he would explain, in the small towns of eastern Europe, wood, coal and water were delivered to people in their homes by small, enterprising businesses.

As my grandfather's story goes, a young lad who worked for one of these businesses was instructed by his boss to deliver a bucket of water to a family who lived at the edge of town. Balancing the bucket on the handlebars of his bicycle, he carefully pedaled the mile and a-half to the customer's home. When he arrived, he knocked on the door. He waited, but no one answered. He knocked again, and waited. After a few minutes, it finally became clear to the boy that no one was home. What should I do, he thought to himself, I've come all this way to deliver water and no one is answering the door. The boss, he remembered, had been very specific. "Don't come back until the water is delivered," he had cautioned. So, believing he was following his boss's instructions, the boy poured the water under the door.

The Legacy of the "Mom and Pop" Shop

Not long ago, I had an experience in a restaurant which taught me something about service. I was greeted at the door, seated and then told it would take a few minutes before my order could be taken because two waitresses had called in sick and the restaurant was shorthanded.

After waiting about 10 minutes, I flagged down a passing waitress and asked whether anyone knew I was there. The waitress explained she would be back to take my order in a few minutes. Another 10 minutes passed. I stopped a bus boy and asked if I could speak to the owner. He told me the owner wasn't there but I could speak to the manager, and pointed to a booth at the rear of the restaurant where two men in suits and ties were having lunch.

I walked over the to the booth and tried to guess which of the two men was the manager. One appeared to be in his mid-twenties, the other seemed about fortyish. They were surrounded by various papers and what seemed to be catalogs of some kind, and I assumed they were in the midst of a working lunch.

I interrupted, "Is one of you the manager?"

The younger man looked up.

"I've been waiting about 20 minutes to place my order," I said, "and I can't seem to get anyone's attention."

The manager smiled and said simply, "We're shorthanded today, sir. Please sit down and we'll get to you just as soon as we can." He took another bite of his lunch and the message was clear—I would get no help from this manager.

I'm a regular customer at "Tarantino's Beyond the Sea," a family-owned Italian restaurant on Milwaukee's East Side. When the lines start forming for the Friday night fish fry, Mama Tarantino, Tony, Paul, Mike the kids and even some of the grandkids instantaneously slip into the roles of waitress, cook, bus boy, dishwasher—whatever is necessary to serve their customers. It doesn't matter who didn't show up for work that day because, at this restaurant, serving the customer always comes first. They understand what it takes to stay in business. They understand that taking care of the customer is the top priority— all of the time.

The legacy of the "Mom and Pop" shop in this country is service. The owners of the business were also the service givers and, almost by definition, they combined the owner's natural interest in preserving the business with the delivery of front-line service. What a powerful combination it is when the person who has contact with the customer also has an interest in the long-term prosperity of the enterprise.

Stop for lunch at Weissgerber's Tavern and Grill at Milwaukee's Third Street Pier and watch Jerry, the daytime bartender, in action. He could teach a graduate level course in giving service. Cheerful, friendly and, still, all business. I'd swear he has eyes in the back of this head—no one walks into the room without having his complete attention. He is fast, he's smooth and he knows how to take care of the customer. He is beautiful to watch. He exemplifies the best of the "Mom and Pop" legacy.

Insurance That Guarantees Tomorrow's Business

In larger organizations, ownership interests must be represented in the company's managers and employees. When their orientation and training does not instill in them the owner's natural understanding that top notch service is the insurance for longevity, that organization is in deep trouble. And what future can there be for employees of a troubled organization?

Think about the last time you went into a restaurant and waited to be noticed while your waiter filled saltshakers or ketchup bottles. It goes beyond irritating, doesn't it? It's as though the waiter or waitress is saying, "I don't care about you. You are not important. I'm just doing my job." Why doesn't he realize you're the reason he has a job?

While no one would disagree that full ketchup bottles and fresh saltshakers are part of good service, these activities are only a means to an end. Folding napkins, polishing silverware and even waiting on tables are simply a means to an end. Tomorrow's business is the desired end. Keeping the customer coming back again and again is the restaurant's real goal. Today's business is assured the moment the customer is seated. After all, won't most people eat and pay the bill even if the food is ordinary and the service poor? What incentive can there be in providing good food and excellent service if it is not to bring the customer back another time?

Good service is insurance for the future. It guarantees tomorrow's business. Restaurant employees—any employees for that matter—who understand this stand the best chance of capturing their bosses' attention and getting promoted. Employees at all levels, from front-line service givers to managers sitting behind desks, need to put the customer first.

What would it take for the clerk at an airline ticket counter to look up every now and then and say to the rest of the people in line, "I know you are there; I'll be with you in just a moment?" Couldn't the ticket clerk go just one tiny step further and with a few simple words indicate the airline actually appreciates that those customers are waiting to give them their business? All it would take is, "Thank you for your patience." It's so simple. "We're glad you're here." It's so powerful. "We appreciate your business." It's so easy, you'd think everyone would do it.

Customers Are Real People

Too many of us hide behind our computers and company policies when dealing with our customers. I remember a particularly difficult situation on a recent business trip. I arrived at the hotel shortly after 11:00 p.m. on a Sunday night. I was very tired. Though I'd made hotel reservations weeks in advance, I had forgotten to bring my computerized reservation form with me. The desk clerk never made eye contact. With her eyes glued to the computer screen, she said in a tone which sounded like a taped message, "I'm sorry, sir, the computer does not show your reservation."

"But, I made a reservation," I explained. "It's almost midnight, are you sure you don't have my reservation?"

"Your reservation is not in the computer. Even if I wanted to, I couldn't' give you a room, sir, because we are full this evening." She explained the city was in the middle of a major national convention and all of the downtown hotels were booked. Nothing I said would help. She kept repeating, "Your reservation is not in the computer," and, "If you made one, it does not show in the computer." I opened my briefcase, whipped out my calendar and showed her where my secretary had written the hotel's name. Again, she said, "I'm very sorry, but as I have told you, sir, your reservation is not here. I'm afraid there's nothing I can do." Her eyes returned to the screen as though I had already disappeared.

From the lobby pay phone, I called a dozen hotels in the area. I was told there were no rooms available. By now, it was almost midnight. I had to be up for an early morning meeting and here I was, in a strange city with no place to sleep. In desperation I telephoned my wife, who got dressed, drove to my office and faxed a copy of my reservation form complete with the original data processing reservation number. When the computerized form was finally produced, the clerk suddenly became "user friendly" and, lo and behold, I was at last ushered to a room. I have no idea where the room came from. I didn't want to know. I can only assume hotel rooms are held in reserve or, perhaps, some poor soul who arrived later than I was left without accommodations.

Service is more than delivering the goods. As in the case of the mysterious disappearing hotel reservation, there are sometimes circumstances which thrust employees into situations over which they have no control. In all fairness, as I look back, I couldn't expect the desk clerk to give me a room if all she had to go on was the information in the computer. The lost reservation was certainly not her fault. She had a job to do under admittedly difficult circumstances.

My problem with the desk clerk was not the fact that my reservation was lost—we all face glitches in life. It was the way I was treated. She refused to look me straight in the eye and deal with me as a human being. She became automatic, distant and machine-like and acted as if I wasn't there. She treated me as though I was just so much furniture that decorated the job each night. That was the problem.

I wanted to be treated like a human being, with courtesy and with understanding. Isn't that the real essence of service? It's not just delivering products in a timely fashion. It's relating to people with a smile, with empathy, with an understanding of what they're feeling and what they need. It's showing respect and protecting their dignity.

Suppose the desk clerk had handled the situation like this:

"I am very sorry, sir. The So and So convention is in town and we are booked solid this evening. I don't doubt that you made a hotel reservation when you said you did, and, certainly, it is entirely possible that our reservation people made this error. But, I sincerely wish you'd brought your confirmation slip with you because we are full and, without some evidence of your reservation, I cannot give you a room.

"With your permission, sir, we'd be happy to try to locate a room for you elsewhere. And, when you return home, if you'll send us a copy of your confirmation, we'll gladly reimburse you for your room. May I try to find another hotel for you, sir?"

With this approach, the desk clerk would have affirmed the possibility that I had made a reservation. And, by gently reminding me that my not getting a room was partly my fault for forgetting my confirmation slip, she would have helped me to appreciate her position—that she had no choice but to decline my request for a room. The key words are respect and dignity. All customers want to feel they are important to the people who provide goods or services in exchange for their money.

Service is the lifeblood of any company. Service should mean one thing and one thing only: Take care of each customer as though the only hope for your personal and professional growth hinges on the way each customer feels when you have finished serving him. Just think about that—then treat every customer who walks into your company's front door as if all of your customers were wrapped up in that one person. This applies even when your job never brings you face to face with a customer. Whether you work in data processing, design, engineering, production, or any other department, keep your sights set on serving your company's customer. Every employee makes a contribution to the company's' ultimate product—its service level.

* * *

Summary

1. Learn and understand your organization's long term goals.
2. Be willing to recognize and revolve conflicts which may arise between policies and long term goals. This will require thinking on your feet and courage to take action.
3. Understand, regardless of written policies and procedures, all companies have one overriding goal: to produce happy customers.
4. If you have the authority to overrule conflicting policies, do so. Otherwise, bring those conflicts to the attention of your supervisor with a suggestion for how to resolve them.
5. Regardless of what you do in the company, try to see how you impact service to your company's customers, and remember, good service insures tomorrow's business.
6. Empathize with your customers. Try to understand their feelings and appreciate their needs. And, always, treat them with respect and dignity.
7. Look after the company's interests and be willing to handle problems in the boss's absence as you believe the boss would handle them.

Chapter 11

Boss Buttering Is Slippery Stuff

> A lie never lives to be old.
> —*Sophocles*

The day came and disappeared quickly as busy days often do. I was on the phone when I looked up and saw Harry Porter standing in the doorway to my office. "Ready?" he asked.

I looked at my watch. It was 5:30 on the button. "You don't waste any time, do you, Harry?"

He smiled.

"Come in and have a seat."

"I've been thinking about our conversations and I think I'm getting the picture," he said, "but there's one thing that still troubles me."

"What's that ?" I asked.

"Well, it seems to me that you've left out a big part. You know, about how a lot of people get promoted by playing politics, buttering up the boss, following him around and licking his shoes . . . well, you know."

Harry had touched a nerve and I knew this was going to be tough. I also knew he was not alone in his thinking. A lot of people believe that promotions go to the boss's favorite employees and not the people who "deserve" them. A lot of employees believe that and, unfortunately, some of the time they are right. The fact is there are bosses who promote people for the wrong reasons in all kinds of organizations. Instead of moving ahead people who help them get the job done, they pick those who make them feel important.

I didn't want Harry to buy into that thinking and wind up deciding that getting ahead amounted to little more than bending at the waist or genuflecting whenever "the boss" passes by. I wanted Harry to understand that playing politics isn't the way it works for most bosses. And, even in those cases where buttering up the boss does work, I wanted him to understand that it's not an effective long term strategy for getting ahead.

I began, "Harry, by allowing yourself to get caught up in this issue, by focusing on how people sometimes get promoted by playing politics, it's easy to avoid the most important reasons employees get ahead."

Harry leaned forward. He put his hands on his knees and stared straight at me. "Are you saying smoothing the boss's fur doesn't help?"

"Well," I said, "that may be the reason some bosses promote people, but it's not the most important one. At least it's not the most important reason for the majority of bosses."

"Then how do you explain Franks's promotion?" he demanded.

Harry had a point. We had recently announced Frank Richards' promotion to a department manager and, quite honestly, I had serious reservations about Frank's ability all along. Frank reported to our retail stores manager who had come to me pushing hard for his promotion. I was distracted at the time by a host of other problems and didn't give his recommendation nearly enough thought. I endorsed it simply because I was busy and wasn't prepared to argue against it.

Harry could sense his question was hard for me to handle and took the opportunity to press the point. "He's hardly what one would call management material, and he's certainly no rocket scientist, and now he's been moved up. Tell me Frank wasn't promoted for reasons that have nothing to do with his qualifications. Tell me there aren't others in the company more qualified. I just want to make the point that sometimes it's not how good you are—it's how much your boss likes you."

"I hate doing it, but I have to agree with you, Harry," I admitted. "Sometimes, it does come down to how much your boss likes you. That shouldn't be the reason people get promoted, but I agree with you that sometimes it is. That doesn't mean you should start your own apple-polishing program."

Harry paused to clear his throat, "Why not? I think Frank is the perfect example of success by apple-polishing," he said. "Frank got promoted because he did just that and he's been at it non-stop for six months. The promotion proves it works. It's his boss's way of paying him back for running errands and agreeing with everything he says." Harry's confidence grew as he spoke. "And what's more," he continued, "I think that's the way it works in a lot of companies. That's what a lot of this company's employees think and, frankly, that's what I think."

A Raise Is a Raise, Isn't it?

I knew he was right. Even in our company, promotions were sometimes given to the people who made their bosses feel important. Yet, I wanted Harry to understand that this belief could keep him from dealing with important issues, those he could do something about, issues he could feel good about years from now.

"I know there are bosses who encourage that kind of thing," I told him, "but I honestly believe those bosses are in the minority. And even they need people who will help them get the job done. There's really only one way to get a meaningful promotion and that's when your boss values your talent and skills and not your bowing and scraping. That's the only healthy situation."

"I just want to move up and make more money," he said. "What difference do the reasons make? Why shouldn't I just give my boss what he wants? If he's looking for strokes, why shouldn't I stroke him?"

Good question, I thought. After all, a promotion is a promotion, isn't it? A raise is a raise. What difference should it make if the promotion is based on merit or stroking the boss?

"Here's the answer," I responded. "Promotions given to reward apple-polishing are hollow imitations of the real thing. They are fraudulent and fleeting, and ultimately they go nowhere, that's the problem. In my estimation, the employee who gets that kind of promotion has no future. He can't help the company grow, and if the enterprise doesn't thrive, what kind of future can there possibly be for the employee—or manager, for that matter?

"But, I want to make sure we don't confuse pandering to the boss with what is perfectly appropriate behavior. It's easy to mistake boss buttering for behavior that is just plain smart."

"Smart?" he questioned.

"Well, let me ask you," I replied. "Is it stroking for an employee to address the boss with courtesy and respect? Is it stroking for an employee to treat the boss with a certain degree of deference?"

Harry wasn't ready to quit. He had a point and he was determined to make sure I heard it. "Isn't it phony for an employee to do things for the boss which are not directly connected to the employee's job description? Let's say, for example, the guy who runs little errands or is always flattering the boss because he knows the boss eats that up—isn't that just so much grease?"

"There's no doubt about it," I said.

"Right on!" Harry replied with obvious satisfaction.

"I admit it's a delicate distinction, Harry," I continued, "but running errands can be appropriate if it improves the boss's ability to produce for the company. There are no hard and fast rules, so it's difficult if not impossible for an employee to know whether running an errand is or is not appropriate. My advice on that one is, if the boss asks, do it.

"As to flattery, when it's contrived and phony, that's pandering, pure and simple. But, what's wrong with a little flattery if it's honest? Bosses, like anyone else, like to be appreciated. Do you know how rare it is for employees to pay a compliment to their boss? Where is it written that compliments should be directed down and never up? I can tell you for a fact, bosses do enjoy compliments from employees when they are honest and legitimate. As long as they aren't false, and aren't given because the employee believes the boss is more interested in being flattered than in getting the job done, I can't see a thing wrong with complimenting the boss now and then.

"Now, I should add that, when flattering is phony, most bosses know it—just like you know it when someone is flattering you dishonestly. That kind of thing doesn't serve an employee's interest. It's really a bogus check, it's a currency that won't buy what you really want."

"So how do you tell the difference?" Harry asked.

Harry had asked the right question. It has a lot to do with the boss's attitude and it's a hard distinction to make. You can start by watching how your boss behaves. For example, if you get the feeling your personal courtesies are expected and taken for granted, if there is an air of class distinction, of social superiority, those are pretty good clues your boss wants to feel important.

When the boss's attitude is appropriate, it's very different. Your courtesies will be returned and appreciated with the same energy and sincerity you express when a favor is done for you. Obviously, it's a much healthier situation when there is give and take, when you are not the only one expected to provide favors. In the best of circumstances, you and your boss are people who, on occasion, do favors for each other.

Moreover, the boss who is not looking to be buttered up is one who will limit the personal favors he or she will accept. This kind of boss will put the organization's welfare first and accept personal favors only on the rarest of occasions. The best employer-employee relationships are ones in which the employee and the boss are equals. I really mean that. They see themselves as deserving of each other's respect. They appreciate their commonality as human beings and understand that they share many of the same needs, aspirations and fears. They are equals who just happen to have different jobs, different responsibilities and, sure, even different salaries.

It's true, however, that many employees still believe the people best liked by their bosses are the ones who get promoted. Take George, for example. George reported to one of our regional middle managers and there's no question in my mind that George got promoted in part because his boss liked him. There were other employees just as qualified, some perhaps more qualified, but George's boss like him better so George won the promotion.

So, what's so unusual or wrong about that? Of course bosses promote people they like. It's human nature. Certainly, bosses don't promote people they don't like. I wouldn't promote a person I didn't like. To get things done, I have to be able to work closely with the people who report to me, and I have to respect them and trust them and like them to do that.

The problem is it's all too easy to generalize from this point and conclude that being liked is everything—that ability doesn't count. That is false. In my own experience, there were a lot of people I liked but wouldn't promote. They had to be able to handle the responsibility of the new job. They had to be capable of performing in the new position. Make no mistake, ability is primary.

Now comes the more difficult question: If my employees were up to it, capable of handling the new responsibilities, and I just didn't like them, what then? Then, in all honesty, I wouldn't promote them. Ability may be primary, but bosses still want to like the people they promote.

A colleague of mine says, "If you have jerks for managers, you guarantee morale problems among employees and damage to relationships with customers." I agreed with him and tried to test for jerkhood in the recruiting process. I attempted to hire people based on what I call the NICE TEAM theory. I wanted people who, first and foremost, were NICE. This, as you can well imagine, was a pretty good test for jerkhood. Then I looked for people who would be TEAM players. That is always a key ingredient in a successful organization. Once these two criteria were met, I looked for people who were "N.I.C.E." (Natural, Intelligent, Courageous and Empathetic). I wanted people who were real—not artificial, people who could think, people who would stand up for what they believed in, and people who could understand and relate to other people's feelings. And, finally, I focused on finding people who where "T.E.A.M." (Trustworthy, Energetic, Ambitious and Motivated).

Bosses like people for various reasons, professional and personal. They like people who are talented, mature and powerful, and who have the talent and skills to perform well. In addition, bosses appreciate many of the same qualities in their employees that many of us like in our friends. They value honesty and sincerity, a sense of humor, the bond of shared common interests, a willingness to lend a hand in friendship, and so on. In short, bosses want to be able to respect and trust the people with whom they work, and they want to enjoy being with them.

But remember, in the final analysis, enjoying another person's company and even being able to respect her or him is not nearly enough if the boss isn't secure with the thought of sharing responsibility. Being able to consider an employee for promotion means believing the employee understands the boss's viewpoint and is capable of getting the job done. Not liking a person may be a good reason *not* to give a promotion, but liking someone is never a good enough reason to give someone a promotion. There's just too much at stake.

Liking Your Boss

Here's the other side of the coin. Employees who want to get ahead also have to like their bosses. Why is that important? Wouldn't I promote a super producer I liked regardless of his or her feeling about me? Put yourself in my shoes. Would you promote an employee who was antagonistic or even cool toward you? Would you feel safe? How could you trust a person who you knew didn't like you? Could you feel comfortable sharing responsibility and working closely with that person? I couldn't. I believe most bosses couldn't.

So, what does an employee do when he thinks his boss is a jerk? Unfortunately, some are. But I think there are many bosses mistakenly perceived as jerks, who are, in fact, pretty good executives who care a lot about their employees' welfare.

Sometimes, believing the boss is a jerk is a convenient excuse for everything that goes wrong. Some employees view their bosses through binoculars turned backwards. They see him or her as a person in another world, someone who could never understand what it's like to be them. These employees are convinced they are very different from their bosses. They think their problems are unique to them and can't imagine their bosses ever having similar problems, or similar hopes and dreams. These are the employees who think of themselves and their fellow employees as "We" and their bosses as "They." And whenever employees form issues in "we-they" terms, real communication is sure to fail.

Give your boss the benefit of the doubt. Even though he or she may have made mistakes or behaved inappropriately, try seeing your boss as a well-intentioned human being who may be temporarily inundated with personal or business problems. To do this, you must be willing to allow that bosses are entitled to make mistakes just like everyone else. Remember, your boss tolerates imperfection from you, so turnabout is only fair.

It's too bad that some bosses are jerks. There's really no cure for having a jerk for a boss. But the possibility of discovering that your boss is a good person with temporary problems, it seems to me, is well worth the effort. Try to find something to like about your boss. Start small if you have to. Maybe you like the way he or she conducts meetings or handles social situations. Make a list of his or her positive qualities and try to focus on those. Also, list his or her negative qualities, but do a reality check on those. Is he or she a jerk all the time, or just some of the time? Give your boss the benefit of the doubt. Let your boss be imperfect.

If the experiment fails, what have you lost? At the very least, you may learn that, in this situation, getting promoted for the right reasons may not be possible. In a later chapter, I discuss what to do if your boss really is a jerk. Until and unless your are absolutely certain of that, however, the smartest strategy for your own sake is to give your boss the benefit of the doubt.

The Outlook for a "Yes-Man"

A corporate executive—we'll call him "Jack"—tells a story that makes the point well. He'd been at a meeting with the company's president and personnel director to discuss their employee compensation system which the personnel director had implemented at the president's direction the year before. Designed to incentivize productivity among senior managers, the plan featured hefty year-end bonuses tied to performance. To accommodate the bonuses to the compensation package, they were accompanied by a virtual freeze on managers' base pay over a two-year period. Now, having been in place for the better part of a year, the new compensation plan was finally beginning to gain acceptance.

In the meeting, the president announced that he was starting to doubt the effectiveness of the new plan which relied so heavily on the year-end bonuses. He suggested that rather than continue the new plan, he was considering going back to the old system where there were no bonuses and base pay was larger. "When base pay was bigger," he declared, "our people seemed to have a better feeling about the company. They felt more secure and there wasn't as much stress at the end of the year. I think we should scrap the current system and go back to what we had." Then, looking straight at the personnel director, the president asked, "What do you think?"

The personnel director, who'd been scribbling comments on a yellow legal pad as the president spoke, looked up from his notes. "Fine," he said. "That sounds fine. We'll have to develop a transition plan of course, and a rationale so the people who have started to appreciate our current system will accept another change without a lot of resistance."

"Good," the president said. "Can you have something in writing in a week or two?" he asked.

"Sure can," the personnel director said, smiling. "Two weeks at the most. Maybe I can have it for you within ten days or so. I'll try."

"That's good," the president replied, and stood up, indicating the meeting was over. Jack and the personnel director got up to leave and as they walked to the door, the president put his hand on the P.D.'s shoulder. "Ten days to two weeks then," he repeated, confirming the assignment.

"Right," was the response.

As the door to the president's office closed behind them, the personnel director looked at Jack and swallowed, struggling to get the words out: "He wants to eliminate the incentives," he blurted. "Damn it anyway, those bonuses work! We've been all through this; I thought we were all together on this. Now he wants to throw away a perfectly good compensation system and go back to a plan that had nothing whatsoever to do with productivity."

Jack was stunned at what he was hearing. He stopped and turned to the personnel director. "If you felt that way about it, why didn't you say so during the meeting? I could have backed you up. You just took notes and nodded affirmations. You even offered to have a transition plan ready in a couple of weeks. I just don't understand."

"Well, it's common sense," the personnel director answered. "The bonuses may not work for everyone, but they're a damn sight better than our old system. And for some of our managers—they work like gang busters. Look at Steinberg and Lazzaro. Look at Whitney. They've been breaking records trying to earn their bonuses. Look at Christianson."

Jack interrupted. "What I'm talking about," he said slowly, "is not whether the bonus plan is better or worse than the old system. That's an issue we'll have to discuss, of course. What I'm talking about right now is why you just sat there in that meeting smiling and agreeing with everything he said when the fact is you really don't agree with him at all. That's what I'm talking about."

"He's the boss, isn't he? He asked me to put a new plan in writing and I agreed to do it. What's wrong with that? I'm just giving him what he wants. Isn't that my role?"

"There's a difference between doing what's asked of you and being honest," Jack replied.

"Listen," the personnel director insisted, "I know what you're say-ing. You're saying the boss doesn't want a lot of 'yes-men' around him. I understand that. But how can I know for certain he doesn't just want me to follow orders and not question them? If I tell him every time I think he's wrong, I'm afraid he might come to see me as the problem. And let me ask you: If he does that, how much would you be willing to bet on my future here?"

This story illustrates how easy it is to misunderstand what bosses really want from their top people. With few exceptions, employees do not serve their bosses by agreeing with everything they say just be-cause they say it. Carrying out instructions when they are given is necessary, but when you're called on to give your opinion, your opin-ion is exactly what the boss wants. He or she wants to know what you think. When the boss makes a decision, he or she wants the benefit of all the available information. If you don't agree with your boss about some action being contemplated, he or she needs to know that.

Admittedly, among the thousands of bosses at all levels there are some who will ask what you think when they really don't want to know. Of course, when your boss says, "I'd like you to do X, Y and Z," there should be no question that you're being asked to follow di-rections. It is much trickier, however, when the boss asks what you think about X, Y and Z. While it may be fair to assume you have a green light to share your honest views when asked for your opinion, I do understand that in some cases it may be difficult to be sure your boss is not just using those words loosely.

In this situation, there *is* something you can do to know with cer-tainty whether your honesty will be welcome. The next time you are asked for your opinion, give it honestly—then listen carefully to the response you get. You should be able to tell from your boss's de-meanor and words whether your advice is welcome. And even if it is not, at least you will have the information to behave appropriately in the future.

One last note: After many conversations with bosses on this subject, I am convinced that, with rare exceptions, the bosses who ask for opinions from their employees do so because they want them. They ask for input because they value it. They know that every business environment is complicated by the noise of competing interests and too many possible courses of action. People in charge need all the good information they can get.

Unfortunately, employees who are honest with their bosses about their views, especially when their opinions seem contradictory, are all too rare. The wise employee, however, will recognize this as an opportunity to become more valuable to their bosses and to their companies as well—and valuable employees are the ones who get promoted.

Learn Your Corporate Culture

Your relationship with your boss is the most critical one you have on the job. If it doesn't work, you may not have a job. And, in the day-to-day course of business life, it helps to have your boss's blessing when you want to sell an idea, resolve a policy dispute or win a budget increase for your department. You need your boss's support when you get into battles with other department heads and you often need his or her endorsement when you want to fire someone. A politician would say that, in your boss, you have a constituency of one. And every political incumbent knows it pays to take care of one's constituency.

Whenever you relate to the boss, you need to think about and keep in mind exactly who it is you are dealing with. It is possible that, by his or her own definition, your boss is a tough, driven, savvy executive who may even admit to being possessed of a big ego (I started this company, I turned it around, etc.) and who is always aware of who is in charge (All things aside, I am the boss). Your boss has the power to hire and fire, to give raises or deny them. Most important of all, your boss has the singular ability to recommend you for a promotion or grant one on his or her own initiative.

Though unintentional, your boss may sometimes mislead you about what he or she wants. That's exactly what happened recently in a large, commercial bank. Having just finished a book which argued that people who focus too much on detail can lose sight of the broad perspective, the bank's senior commercial loan executive wrote a memo to her mangers with instructions that, in the future, they were to abbreviate and summarize rather than write reports filled with minutiae.

One astute manager noticed that in spite of this instruction, the executive continued to do her own work with meticulous attention to detail. He recognized this did not square with the memo he received and decided to trust his instincts rather than take the memo literally. Accordingly, he continued to include substantial detail in his reports and, as he expected, they were well received by the bank executive while other managers were repeatedly asked to provide additional detail.

Learn to get along with your boss's staff. Much of the boss's view of you is shaped by what his staff reports to him. Treat the boss's secretary with the same courtesy you give the boss. Do it because it is the right thing to do. Also do it because the boss's secretary can be a useful ally. Remember, the boss's secretary has immediate access to the boss every day—you don't. And make it your business to know who your boss's husband or wife is and always treat him or her with courtesy and respect. On more than one social occasion, I've seen my wife nudged aside by a well-intentioned employee anxious to shake hands and have me meet his spouse or date.

Learn to read your boss. Look for signals you can use to understand what your boss really wants. Know what makes your boss happy and be responsive. If your boss is meticulously detailed, understand that he or she values detail and behave accordingly. If he or she prefers short memos, don't write novels. Unless your boss responds to memos with a handwritten scribble across it's face, your notes should be typed and formal. If punctuality is important to your boss, try to be on time. If he or she doesn't use profanity, avoid the use of four-letter words in your own speech.

Figure out how your boss likes to communicate. Is he or she a telephone person or a face-to-face communicator. Does he or she like meetings or prefer discussion one-on-one? How does your boss learn? Is he or she a reader or a talker? If your boss is a reader, deliver your message in writing; if he's a talker, your best bet may be to make regular appointments and sit down across the desk from him, In the latter case, you'll want to determine the best times to catch your boss for a short meeting. Is he or she generally available to talk to first thing in the morning or are afternoons a better bet?

Does your boss maintain an "open door" to employees on all but rare occasions? If so, keep the door to your own office open most of the time. If your boss likes to manage by walking around, make it your business to get around the office or plant and know what's happening "out there." If your boss is visibly engaged in numerous charitable endeavors, you have reason to feel comfortable increasing your own involvement in community service activities. Be on the alert for cues about what makes your boss tick and develop a style that fits.

It is the wise employee who is aware of how the boss behaves in and out of the office. I'm not suggesting you should copy the boss in everything he or she does. I'm saying it's smart to avoid doing things that contradict your boss's preferences or is incongruent with your boss's style. Observe the boss for clues about how to behave. Whether intentional or not, your boss has developed a style, a bearing, an atmosphere and a corporate culture in which he or she is comfortable working. It's smart to watch your boss in action and learn how he or she relates to people and reacts to issues. It's understandable you will want to develop a style of your own, but develop one which is compatible with your corporate culture.

* * *

Summary

1. Know that promotions won by flattery and boss buttering ultimately go nowhere.
2. Recognize that your work environment is unhealthy if you are routinely expected to do personal favors for your boss that have nothing to do with the welfare of the company.
3. Recognize that your work environment is healthy if your boss limits personal favors requested of you, and seems willing to reciprocate from time to time.
4. Don't confuse boss buttering with smart behavior. It's smart to act in ways that please your boss. Address him or her with courtesy and respect, and remember, bosses, like anyone else, like to hear they are appreciated and enjoy compliments from employees when they are honest and deserved.
5. There's nothing wrong with being liked by the boss. Ability may be primary, but bosses still want to like the people they promote.

Chapter 12

Sex in the Office and Other Ethical Dilemmas

Common-sense in an uncommon degree is what the world calls wisdom.

—*Samuel Coleridge*

Ethics in the workplace is a hot topic, and it ought to be. Rarely a week passes when the nation's newspapers and TV networks aren't describing the sordid details of one scandal or another. Last week, another politician's career went down the drain. The week before that, a religious leader was facing charges of embezzlement and fraud. It's pervasive. From insider trading on Wall Street to scandals in the White House, Congress, the Pentagon and recently at HUD, we are inundated with news of others' wrongdoing. It's no wonder we have trouble knowing what is ethical behavior and what is not.

We don't teach ethics in grade school, much less in high school. We ought to. It's important to people personally, and it's important in business. I also think it helps people get promoted. Bosses really do appreciate people who are ethical.

Now I know that a lot of people think business is unethical to begin with. Lots of folks think business people are just in it for the buck. That's the image—in the press, on television and in the movies. Business people are portrayed as greedy and insensitive, almost never in a positive way. And since the media tend to reflect wider attitudes in the country, this anti-business bias troubles me, as it troubles most bosses, a great deal.

With rare exception, my experience in business and with business people has been different. Sure, there's a strong focus on being profitable, on beating the competition and on winning business. In business, we are motivated to achieve and succeed. But I have always been impressed with the number of top executives who are committed to operating ethically, and who have a profound social conscience. Most executives, I believe, are convinced that ethical behavior is in their companies' long-term best interest. That is my belief. I don't deny there have been glaring and widely publicized exceptions to the rule, but my experience is that people in business do care very much about ethics.

In 1902, believing strongly in a high standard of ethical conduct in business, James Cash Penney, founder of the J.C. Penney Company, named his first store The Golden Rule: "Do unto others as you would have them do unto you." What American child hasn't learned the Golden Rule in school?

The problem is, while the Golden Rule is a pretty good lesson for kids, it provides little direction for dealing with the ethical problems we face as adults. Penney and his partners must have realized that because, in 1913, they developed a set of written principles of ethical conduct for Penney employees which, notably, is still cited today in the Code of Ethics for Penney Employees.

The Penney code encouraged employees to: " . . . Test our every policy, method and act in this [way]: Does it square with what is right and just?"

Sounds pretty good, but it presumes that everyone, in every situation, will know what is "right and just." The problem is the circumstances one faces from day to day are much too varied for that. For example, take the matter of employees who are engaged in a romantic relationship.

If one or both of them are married, then, certainly, the relationship is unethical.

If neither one is married, then I would ask if one person reports to the other. If that is the case, the relationship is unethical because it damages the boss's ability to be impartial. Almost by definition, the boss has the authority to make rules and the resources to enforce them. That is the definition of power, and when a boss becomes involved in a relationship with an employee, it puts him or her in a compromising situation. This kind of relationship can lead to the unfair use of that power, which is, in itself, unethical.

But is it unethical if the boss doesn't abuse his or her authority? Yes it is. Is it unethical from the start. Just being in a situation where favoritism is possible is unethical. It's not just the actual abuse of power by a boss, it's the potential for abuse which arises from a conflict of interest which is unethical. Sometimes, even the appearance of a conflict of interest can be every bit as damaging as a bona fide conflict and should, therefore, be avoided.

It's no different in other professions. A United States Senator can't own stock in a corporation which could benefit from legislation on which he is working. Lawyers can't represent both parties in a controversy. And they can't talk privately to members of the jury while a trial is in progress, even if they never discuss the trial. It's the mere potential for compromising impartiality which makes a conflict of interest unethical.

So, as long as neither person is married and one of them isn't the boss, is it fair to deduce that a relationship between them would be O.K.? Not exactly. Impartiality can also be compromised in a relationship between peers, especially when they work in the same department or on the same projects. The problem is that amorous relationships between fellow employees often lead to conflicts that can severely impair the performance of one of the employees, or both. Take, for example, what happened to Freddie Sonya and Maria Bernard.

Here were two unmarried co-workers who became romantically involved. At first, everyone thought their relationship would last forever. But, then, as often happens, they had a lovers' quarrel and went weeks without talking to one another. It disrupted the whole department. When relationships go sour, they can affect a large part of the company and result in the loss of good people. Freddie and Maria's relationship didn't last and, in the end, we lost them both. Maria said she couldn't work around Freddie anymore and started looking for another job. She was gone inside a month. Freddie was embarrassed by the whole thing and left a short time later.

It was sad. I liked them. More important, at one time they were two very effective, productive people, good for the company. It hurt to lose them. It hurt our company and it hurt them. The unfortunate thing from their standpoint is, because they allowed themselves to get into a relationship at work, they got to the point where they believed they had no alternative but to give up their jobs, jobs they were good at, jobs they liked.

I wasn't born yesterday. Affairs between employees have been going on since companies were organized and people of opposite sexes started working together. From my point of view, what people do on their own time is their business—until what they do starts to affect their work.

Fearful of personal relationships which may impair productivity, more and more companies are instituting policies prohibiting intimate relationships between employees. But, whether or not a formal policy exists, there is a final reason why employees ought to avoid romantic relationships with other employees. It goes beyond conflicts of interest and the potential for losing one's impartiality. It has to do with getting promoted.

Whether having an amorous interest at work actually affects an employee's ability to focus, to concentrate on the tasks at hand, deal with the company's problems, think with clarity and give undivided attention to the job, that is often the impression left with co-workers and bosses. This is a case where reality counts less than the perception of reality on the part of co-workers and bosses. The long and short of it is this: Bosses don't promote people who are romantically involved with another employee or have a reputation for becoming involved with other employees, because bosses don't promote people who aren't all business.

Ethical dilemmas in the business arena take so many different shapes and occur in so many different settings, they can be confusing and difficult to deal with. I know—I've made my share of mistakes over the years.

What ethical problems have in common is they always involve some level of competition between the employee's interests and those of the company, its representatives, customers or other employees. And they always involve a potential violation of trust. Let me give you an example.

Living in a "Dog-Eat-Dog" World

A labor lawyer I know tells the amazing story of a woman who became the highest paid executive secretary in a fairly sizable corporation only to be fired later on grounds of incompetency.

She started in the firm at an entry level position but, unlike most of her peers, was communicative about wanting to move up. And move up she did. Her boss gave her extremely high marks on three successive performance evaluations, noting on the last: "She has excellent skills and is very interested in advancement opportunities within the company." With apparent generosity, he added a personal note recommending her for promotion. Shortly thereafter, she received an invitation from a vice president in another division asking if she would be willing to transfer to a new job with a substantial increase in salary. Of course, wanting to grow, she accepted.

Her performance evaluations remained excellent and she continued to express interest in advancement. Within a few years, she was invited to accept another promotion and, like the time before, this one would also involve a move to another division where she would work for still another new boss. Again, she would benefit from a nice bump in salary.

She began to believe she'd discovered the formula for getting ahead. She did her job the best she could and continued to show interest in moving up. This time, she didn't have to wait long. Within 18 months, she was promoted still another time. In all, she received five promotions over a period of 11 years. Each promotion took her to a new boss, and each was accompanied by a slightly new title and a substantial raise in pay. How could she have known she was on her way to being fired?

In the subsequent unfair labor action, her attorney argued she had been fired inappropriately. He said the firm could not justify her termination on grounds of incompetency when, in fact, it had established a clear record of excellent performance evidenced by her many promotions and pay raises. This was proof, the attorney said, that she must have been good at her job and a very fine secretary.

The attorney told me privately, however, that in actual fact this secretary had minimal skills. He had personally tested her and found she was unable to type in excess of 35 words per minute. He said she plunked at the typewriter stopping frequently to paint over errors with correction fluid. Also, he said, she had never learned to use her company's sophisticated copy machines and admitted to being entirely overwhelmed by its word processing equipment. "Those," the lawyer said, "were the facts."

"How then," I asked, "was it possible for so incompetent an individual to win all those promotions?"

The lawyer explained that, except for her last boss—the one who fired her—all the others used her performance evaluation as a device for getting rid of an undesirable employee. Wanting to avoid the distasteful task of having to terminate a well-intentioned and established employee, they used a ploy to entice their colleagues to hire the problem away.

Here's how it worked: With glowing reports, each boss set up the next, encouraging the belief that she was a very fine secretary with excellent skills. As each boss discovered he'd been duped, he concluded (mistakenly, I might add) that, in this dog-eat-dog world of "big business," it is acceptable to "do unto others as they [have done] unto you." One after another, they misled, they fabricated, they exaggerated until, finally, one executive looked at his secretary and realized she was not performing her duties. Not knowing he'd been misled by the series of fraudulent performance reports, he concluded she was either goldbricking or, for some reason he didn't understand, wanted to get fired. And so, he decided to accommodate her. He fired her.

The employee filed an action and, appropriately, won her lawsuit against the corporation. She was compensated with damages sufficient to enable her to acquire retraining and, in the meantime, maintain the lifestyle to which the company had enabled her to become accustomed.

On learning the details about how several of his managers had participated in this tragedy of errors, the company's president fired the executives involved, and published the following memo:

TO ALL EMPLOYEES . . .

Ladies and Gentlemen:

By this time, no doubt, everyone has heard about the recent termination of four of our executives.

I understand that many of you are wondering why these longtime employees were fired. Simply put, they lost their jobs because they willfully exaggerated information in company personnel reports and did so for their personal benefit. Though they did not intend monetary gain, they benefitted from their actions nevertheless, and caused extreme hardship and suffering to an innocent employee who had no way to prevent herself from being involved in these regrettable circumstances.

It is always sad to lose quality people for any reason much less for what may appear to be an extremely minor infraction of just one company rule. That we behave in all of our dealings with honesty and integrity, however, is much more than that. It is a rule of ethical conduct which is regarded throughout our society as essential to the survival of human decency, and this company sees it no differently.

With this memo, therefore, I want to make it clear that dishonesty in any form will not be tolerated in this organization. Further, it is the philosophy of this company that we are our brothers' keepers, even in the workplace.

I trust we have learned something worthwhile from this unfortunate incident and hope we can look back on it with a better sense of the limits within which we must all live and work. I am confident we will proceed with the same energy and purpose which has made our company great.

Very sincerely

President

With this memo, the president made clear his belief that the rules one lives by in one's private life must be carried into the workplace. We are no less responsible for our actions because we are "out there" in the "cruel world."

Stealing Ideas and Other Intangibles

The senior executive for a widely known retail clothing chain told me the following story. One morning shortly after this executive was hired, the president of the company called a meeting of vice presidents and other senior staff people to discuss procedures for adding new stores.

One of the vice presidents, we'll call him Blaine, asked the company president if he had seen the quality of the start-up material being sent to new stores. Blaine was emphatic. "I mean, they're just awful. Have you seen the stuff we're sending out?"

The president frankly admitted he hadn't, to which Blaine quickly replied, "Well, I've got an idea. Why don't you have a box of the literature sent directly to you. And," he emphasized, "I don't mean sent to you as the president of the company—I mean sent to you anonymously so you can get a first-hand look at the garbage our stores are getting from the home office." The president was concerned about the caliber of intra-company communications and thought this was an idea worth pursuing. He made a note to follow through.

Later that day, the executive was talking with one of the company's middle managers who had not been present at the meeting. The manager remarked that he had what he thought was a pretty good idea. He explained that the start-up materials the company was sending to new stores were, in his opinion, outdated and extremely disorganized, and he thought if the president were to get a box just as the stores get them, there would soon be a directive to improve them.

Of course, the executive instantly recognized Blaine's idea from the morning meeting. He asked, "Have you mentioned this to anyone else?"

"Yes," the manger replied, "I told Blaine about it yesterday."

Certainly, the manager should have gotten the credit for his own idea. He shouldn't have had it stolen by Blaine. I asked the executive if he told the president who's idea it really was.

"As a matter of fact, I didn't," he said. He explained he had recently come on board and didn't yet know the people involved or fully understand the relationship between Blaine and the president. So, he had to decide how important this issue was relative to everything else: his own welfare, the company's welfare. He had to decide whether it was worth the risk to fight this battle. He decided it wasn't. "This wasn't the ditch I was going to die in," he said.

I suppose one could fault his ethics by stretching the point. But, personally, I didn't blame him for stepping lightly in that situation. It's not black and white. It never is. I don't have all the answers by a long shot but it seems to me that, while we are our brothers' keepers, we can't make other people's welfare our personal responsibility at any price whatsoever. What we can do is behave in ways that never intentionally or knowingly offend or diminish another person's rights.

But let's assume something for a minute. Let's assume that Blaine got away with it, that the president never found out the idea was stolen and continued to think it was Blaine's idea. Would Blaine have scored more points getting credit for the idea or by being honest and giving the manager credit?

Bosses want people with good ideas but the ability to be a team player and a team builder is much more valuable than a good idea here and there. I like good ideas just as most bosses do, but running a company effectively requires management that excites and involves its people. The principle objective of organizational management is, after all, to get things done.

Suppose, in that meeting, Blaine had said something like this: "I was talking to one of our managers yesterday—his name, by the way, is Tony Molly— and he had what I thought was one hell of an idea. Now I don't want to steal Tony's thunder, but the idea was so good I don't think he'd mind if I shared it with you here."

It does feel better, doesn't it? Blaine is more likable and he would have scored more points with the president on a number of counts: for integrity, for getting around the plant to talk with employees about the company's problems and, also, for being able to recognize a good idea when he heard one. In the end, Blain's credibility with the boss would have gone up by several degrees, and that's worth more than an occasional good idea any day. Credibility and trust go together, and bosses promote people they trust.

The purchasing agent who accepts dinners, gifts or other things of value in exchange for favoring a particular supplier sacrifices the company's legitimate interest in making purchasing decisions based exclusively upon performance, the merits of the product and price. It's a violation of the company's trust.

The executive who runs personal errands on company time cheats the company (and, indirectly, all employees who depend upon its prosperity) of its interest in receiving honest value for its salary dollar. That's a violation of trust.

The salesperson who pads an expense account, the bookkeeper who hurries past detail, the chef who takes steaks home, the receiving clerk who doesn't check orders thoroughly, the office worker who is careless with supplies, the trainer who takes shortcuts during preparation, the personnel director who doesn't check references, the night security officer who sleeps on the job, and the supervisor who accepts anything in exchange for favoritism—all these are examples of persons serving their own interests at the expense of the legitimate interest of the company and other employees. In its simplest terms, this behavior is a violation of trust and, therefore, unethical.

Admittedly, these are relatively easy-to-recognize examples of behavior which do not "square with what is right and just." Often, however, what is "right and just" is not so easy to discern.

The Conflict Predicament

Take, for example, the situation in which Aria Kim found herself. Aria was a physical therapist employed by a retailer of medical equipment and supplies. An aging woman had just been released from the hospital after suffering a hip fracture, and Aria was asked to visit the patient's home to make a medical equipment needs assessment. It was her job to recommend medical equipment which would make the patient's stay at home feasible and, also, more comfortable. Among other things, Aria determined the woman would need a wheelchair.

Aria's company carried wheelchairs from about five different manufacturers, which meant she could choose from well over 250 wheelchair models. She knew that was an exceptional variety by industry standards, yet she believed the best wheelchair was not one of those represented in her company's inventory. The best wheelchair for this particular person, Aria believed, was one carried by a competitor.

Aria Kim was facing a dilemma—an ethical dilemma. Should she deliver a wheelchair from her company and come close to providing what the customer needed, or should she refer the customer to a competitor?

An argument can be made that Aria's first obligation was to her own company. She was, after all, employed as her company's representative and paid to provide service to her company's customers. Could she then, in good conscience, make a referral to a competitor? Wouldn't she be violating her company's trust? Aria Kim was deeply troubled. She knew these were not easy questions to answer.

An employee's primary responsibility is, of course, to his or her employer. Being employed is more than a relationship of trust, it is a contract. By accepting a position on the company's payroll, an employee is obligated to perform in the company's interest. This obligation to perform in the company's interest is universal, providing such performance does not violate the law. And no one would argue that Aria would violate the law by recommending her company's product, even though she believed it to be inferior. The question is, would such a recommendation violate a principle of ethics?

Because this is a health related matter, I believe the only ethical thing Aria could have done was to recommend the competitor's wheelchair. The guidepost for Aria in this case had to be her ethics and standards as a health professional. She had obligations to her profession and to society as a whole, which superseded her obligations to the company.

On hearing this suggestion that there are occasions where an employee might have obligations beyond those to the company, not all bosses will agree with me. I can almost hear some of them now. "You did WHAT? You sent our customer WHERE?" Some bosses would go crazy.

Well, maybe. Bosses are human beings too. But most bosses know that various professions have codes of ethics and appreciate their value to society. They also know there are many ways Aria could have handled this situation.

If she had explained to the customer that, while her company had many different types of wheelchairs any number of which might be nearly perfect, the customer should know about a competitor's product which might better meet her needs. Then, if the customer still preferred to have Aria's company provide the wheelchair, Aira could have proceeded on her company's behalf with a clear conscience.

Apart from questions of ethics, recommending the competitor's product in this instance might also have been the smart thing for Aria to do. After all, taking care of the customer's interest is usually in the company's long term interest. Ethical companies don't just care about todays' business—they care about tomorrow's.

And, isn't it likely that the credibility of Aria's company would have been enhanced in the customer's mind by Aria's honesty? Wouldn't the customer have developed a higher level of confidence and trust in Aria and in her company that would bring her back to meet future needs? Taking care of the customer is usually in the company's interest.

This kind of ethical dilemma is typical of those faced by other health professionals, as well as social workers, lawyers, architects, account-ants and teachers, to name a few. Taking care of the customer is ulti-mately in the interest of business but, if Aria were selling TV sets or stereos instead of medical equipment, her obligation to her company's interest might have superseded her obligation to the customer. Ours is a free enterprise economy and *Caveat Emptor* (Buyer Beware) is still the accepted rule, though pro-consumer legislation of the last 10 to 15 years has increasingly required sellers to take responsibility for con-sumer safety.

"Buyer Beware"

It is unethical for a stereo salesman to sell a product he knows has a wiring defect and could be a fire hazard. If a product is dangerous, it is unethical to promote it as safe. Fraud is always unethical. But is it unethical for that stereo salesman to sell a safe product which he knows to be safe but believes is inferior to other products in other ways? That is a much tougher question.

Certainly, he can't promote his product as better or even equal to other products if he knows it isn't. Telling lies about a product is fraud and fraud is not only unethical, it is illegal. But, what if he doesn't lie about his product's advantages and simply withholds from the cus-tomer his personal belief that his product is inferior? Does this violate a rule of ethics?

All of us want to be doing things we believe in and, to the extent we can, we ought to. Apart from that, however, a salesman should not have an ethical problem selling his company's products with enthusi-asm and energy as long as he is honest and aboveboard with cus-tomers—yes, even if he, himself, would not buy the product.

First of all, what that stereo salesman may think is superior may not match what an engineer thinks or, for that matter, what the consumer thinks. One person may rate the stereo based on speaker quality, an-other on cabinet construction, and still another person may prefer to value styling. What the salesman can ethically do—and I realize others may not agree with me—is describe his product's attributes without exaggeration or false comparison and leave the choice to the customer.

We live in a free enterprise economy which is based on competition. That means companies compete with each other for the consumer's business. Providing, of course, that all laws are obeyed and the seller does not violate his personal ethics or the ethics of his profession, in our society it's up to the consumer to make choices. For example, the seller must follow all labeling laws but it's the consumer's responsibility to read them.

Twelve Rules of Ethics in Business

Over the years, I have identified 12 rules of ethical conduct which, I believe, cover the majority of ethical problems an employee can face in the workplace.

First, there are five Primary Rules which concern the company's behavior or the behavior of employees when they are operating on the company's behalf.

PRIMARY RULES OF BUSINESS ETHICS:

1. Give your customers value for their dollar.
2. Obey all federal, state and local laws.
3. Protect company property, both tangible and intangible, against internal and external theft or misuse.
4. Learn to recognize conflicts of interest where they exist and always preserve the company's interest over competing interests, including your own.
5. Treat all people, customers as well as those who report to you, with equity, and without bias as to race, color, ethnic origin, religion, sex, age or disability.

In addition to the five Primary Rules, there are seven Personal Rules that relate to an employee's personal behavior.

Personal Rules of Business Ethics

1. Never lie.
2. Live up to promises you make to your boss and to those who report to you.
3. Whenever you accept the trust of your boss or of those who report to you, never violate that trust.
4. Protect and defend the reputations of both your company and your boss inside and outside the organization.
5. Be honest about crediting others when credit is due.
6. Avoid romantic relationships with fellow employees.
7. Give your company value for its dollar.

These rules, while they are certainly appropriate guidelines for personal ethical conduct, also impact the boss's ability to trust an employee—and bosses will not promote people they don't trust. Given the wide variety of circumstances which may raise questions of ethics, my final suggestion is this: If you are unsure about whether a contemplated action is ethical, get input from your peers, and don't hesitate to ask your boss. The best rule always is:

IF YOU'RE NOT SURE, ASK.

*   *   *

Summary

1. Amorous relationships between the boss and an employee are always unethical. A relationship between employees can be unethical if it affects their work or presents one or both of them with a potential conflict of interests.
2. Romantic relationships between employees damages their ability to get promoted because bosses believe such relationships create the potential for problems. In this case, perception can be as damaging as reality.

3. Most bosses believe individuals are no less responsible for their actions in the working world than they are in their private lives.

4. Credibility and trust go together, and bosses promote people they trust.

5. While employees have a contractual obligation to their employers, the law and other principles of ethics should take precedent.

6. Learn to recognize conflicts of interest where they exist and always preserve the company's interest over competing interest, including your own.

7. Live up to the promises you make to your boss, those who report to you, and your customers.

8. Give your company value for its dollar. Give your customers value for their dollar.

9. Protect and defend the reputations of both your company and your boss inside and outside the organization.

10. If you're not sure about a question of ethics, don't hesitate to ask.

Chapter 13

Criticism—The Art of Give and Take

To be criticized is not necessarily to be wrong.
—*Sir Anthony Eden*

Criticism is like bad news: Few of us are good at giving it and nobody likes to receive it. Giving and receiving criticism is, however, a necessary part of working for people and having people work for you. Praise may be effective reinforcing successful performance, but criticism is the most direct way to correct undesirable behavior. It is virtually impossible to hold a job without receiving criticism at one time or other. It's normal. It goes with the territory and, since criticism is a part of every working experience, we must all learn to handle it well and benefit from it.

But people are not robots. Criticism never feels good and can be downright threatening. When criticized, most of us pull back as though we've just touched a hot stove. It's involuntary. It's instinctive. We withdraw and get defensive to avoid being hurt. We have all experienced feelings of inadequacy in our lives, and criticism threatens to renew them. The problem is, when threatened, we sometimes stop thinking. And, when we stop thinking, we are left to draw on old emotions which can lead to knee jerk responses that can damage our ability to win promotions.

As I think about the employees who have worked for us, three come to mind who were notably poor at taking criticism. Neal Banks couldn't take criticism at all. He was an excuse maker. It was always someone else's fault. Any time I criticized Neal I was instantly met with a rapid, run-on sentence brimming with explanation. Either he had been misinformed, or he couldn't do it because more important things needed doing, or another executive gave him different instructions, or his father was extremely ill and had to be rushed to the hospital—always at the last minute, always in an emergency.

By my calculation, Neal's father spent more time in the hospital than the hospital administrator. The day I finally met him, I was amazed at how healthy and vibrant this man of 80 was. He walked with zest and talked with energy that wouldn't quit. Given the frequent episodes of hospitalization, Neal's father was a marvel of modern medicine by any standard. Either that, or Neal wasn't telling the truth. In Neal's mind, however, there was never the slightest possibility his excuses weren't legitimate. He had himself convinced. Unfortunately for Neal, he didn't fool anyone else.

Nancy Goldman was also memorable. She reacted to criticism in a different way. She got blood-boiling mad. In response, she delivered criticisms of her own. She believed the best defense is a good offense. Like a hardened combat veteran, she would fire off rounds of the stuff in a flurry that would make one's head spin.

"Nancy," her boss would say, "you are three days late with that sales report. I had other people scheduled to work on it and now their work has to be postponed. This delay is costly to the company, so please have it on my desk by the end of the week."

Nancy would bristle. "Why didn't you tell me it was that important? Last month, I delivered my report on time and then it sat on your desk for a week. It's impossible to know what you want when you're so inconsistent. It's not right. It's not fair. Why should I be on time with things if nobody else is? And by the way, where are those new brochures you promised?"

Arthur Perkins took criticism in still another way. Arthur would get quiet, his face would redden and his lips tighten into a squinched pout. He'd fold his arms across his chest and drop his chin as if to protect himself from injury. Though he didn't like criticism, Arthur took it. He took it dutifully, subserviently. However unhappy it made him, he reacted with deference and respect for authority as though it was part of his job. He believed he owed that to any individual higher in rank than he.

And it was temporary, he told himself. After all, he had more authority than some people in the company and later he could pass his anger and frustration on to them. When later came, he spared no one. He spread criticism around with gusto. It made him feel better, using the chain of command in that way. It helped him get rid of the feelings of anger he felt when he was criticized.

The Art of Receiving Criticism

The ability to take criticism well is especially important to employees who want to be promoted. It can help them tune in to the needs and spirit of the company, and demonstrate the maturity bosses want and expect from their employees. The trick in learning to take criticism well is to keep thinking, and the key to that is believing in yourself, believing in your ability and value to the enterprise. When one feels good about one's self, criticism is less likely to elicit the emotions which inhibit thinking.

Russell Lynne's story is a good example. He was hired as a junior level marketing assistant by a manufacturer of industrial chemicals. An effective employee, Russell was promoted twice in four years and eventually became Director of Product Development. In that capacity, Russell had the primary responsibility for surveying and evaluating customer reaction to new products after they were introduced in the market.

Most of his work was done by direct mail and telephone. On occasion, however, he was expected to visit customers in person and interview them face-to-face, which meant he had to travel on business. This took him out of the city approximately two days every other week.

Russell didn't particularly like traveling. So, to make his trips more enjoyable, he scheduled them on Mondays and Fridays. This meant they would coincide with weekends which enabled him to organize Saturday and Sunday visits with out-of-town friends. Utilizing company paid air travel to make personal visits in this way, he thought, was a really nice perk.

Aware of his company's concern about escalating travel costs, Russell was meticulous in making sure company money was never spent on anything not directly beneficial to the company. In spite of this careful planning, Russell Lynne was due for a surprise.

One morning, Harriet Blake, Vice President of Marketing and Russell's boss, asked him to come to her office prepared to clarify the reasons his business trips were always scheduled on Mondays and Fridays.

"I thought it wouldn't matter as long as it didn't cost the company anything," Russell explained. "I fly in first thing Friday morning, have business meetings all day and check into a hotel later that night. And always," he emphasized, "I check out of the hotel on Saturday morning and check back in again on my personal credit card, so Saturday and Sunday night are always charged to me. That way, because I'm on a flight home Monday night, it only costs the company for one night's lodging. Also," he added, "I pay for all my own meals and other expenses on weekends."

"I appreciate the way you've handled expenses, Russell," she replied, "but you're gone on Mondays and Fridays and those are the two busiest days of the week. That's not O.K. When questions come up, we want you here."

Criticism makes us all stop. Our brain tells us we're under attack. We need reaction time. We want to get a grip. We want to concentrate and not miss a thing. We want to let it sink in.

Russell's mind raced. He could hear her voice: "That's not O.K. When questions come up, we want you here."

"Damn it!" he thought. "I've gone to all this trouble to make sure it wouldn't cost the company anything, and now they say it's not O.K. Besides, I hate traveling!"

Then something very important happened. Russell's thinking switched gears. "Wait a minute," he thought. "She said they need me."

Again, he replayed her words: "When questions come up, Russell, we want you here." He could hear her voice so clearly now, "'Mondays and Fridays . . . the two busiest days of the week.'"

"Sure," he thought. "It's true. Mondays are always crazy around this place. Everybody's catching up from the weekend. And Fridays . . . Fridays are nuts too."

He took a deep breath and let it out slowly. He was beginning to understand what his boss had been saying. It was becoming clearer, making sense. "It's not the money at all," he thought. "They're not accusing me of anything. The issue is simple: They need me here."

It seemed like minutes, but he realized only seconds had passed. He looked at his boss, sitting there, patient and serious, waiting for his reply. Finally, he smiled and said, "I understand. As I think about it, it does make sense. I appreciate your telling me, and I'll make certain my travel does not take me out of the office on Mondays and Fridays. You can count on that."

"Thank you, Russell," she replied. "That will help a lot."

"No sweat," he said. "If there's anything else you'd like me to do differently, you just let me know."

Harriet Blake was genuinely pleased he was able to understand the company's point of view, and do it so quickly. It was obvious he'd engineered a considerable personal benefit from his business travel, and was now willing to give it up. Many employees, she knew, wouldn't react so evenly and rationally. She made a mental note about him—an even temper and rational behavior were qualities she looked for in people. They were qualities she wanted in the people she would promote.

Russell Lynne understood mostly from this encounter the value in criticism. He viewed it as useful feedback from which he could learn how to give his boss and his company what was wanted. Sure, like the rest of us, he got a little off balance at first. But then, after getting his footing, after thinking through the criticism's content, he approached it without defenses, without anger, and with a sincere willingness to understand what changes his boss wanted. He learned to make himself a better and more effective employee by accepting criticism with an open mind.

The key to turning criticism into a beneficial learning experience is to relax and let go of your natural defenses. Open up, be receptive and think. Consider all the elements of the criticism you receive and ask yourself truthfully, "Is there anything valid in what has been said? Is there any part of the criticism I have received which accurately describes my behavior? What is the behavior my boss really wants?" This kind of thoughtful consideration of the criticism you receive will turn into a powerful force for change which can do nothing but help you get promoted.

The Art of Giving Criticism

Criticism is a powerful thing. Even when whispered, it is always loud to the person receiving it. When the boss is speaking, employees instinctively turn the volume up. Unfortunately, that's more true about criticism than it is about praise. A colleague who well understands the difference shares this management bromide: "Give 'em one hundred 'Atta-Boys' for every 'Aw Shit!'"

Since almost all employees who want to get promoted have or hope to have people reporting to them, it is important to know how to give criticism. The one criticizing has a great responsibility since, depending on how it is given, criticism can be either constructive or destructive. It can help an employee understand what's wrong and even give a recipe for fixing it, or it can elicit feelings of fear, resentment and anger. There is no place for criticism unless it clearly describes the problem and provides instruction on how to do things better. Criticism which merely inventories what is wrong is almost always counterproductive. Worse, it's demoralizing to the one receiving it. It destroys confidence, saps energy and initiative, and it can literally destroy a potentially great contributor.

Among the several employees of mine who were particularly poor at giving criticism, Scott Jones was the worst. He was sarcastic and often brutally personal, having reduced more than one employee to tears before completing his list of offenses. "For heaven's sake, Louise," he would say, "why aren't you following directions? How often do I have to tell you what I want from you? You're not thinking half the time. Maybe you're not getting enough sleep or something. Get your act together, Louise, or you're out of here!"

If that wasn't bad enough, Scott Jones committed the gravest of managerial sins. Where there was something about an employee's behavior he didn't like, he reacted visibly without regard to who might be around at the time. Once, in full view of others, I caught him grimacing and clawing the air behind an employee who had just questioned an assignment. I had no choice but to let him go and did it that afternoon.

Obviously, Scott Jones did not have the maturity and personality to manage people. Most bosses know that effective team building is critically important in any organization. They know it takes energized people to get things done and, for this reason, value highly managers who are effective at motivating others. If you want to get ahead in your organization, know this: How you give criticism to those who report to you can make or break your own chances for success. Giving criticism is an integral part of managing others, and bosses don't promote employees who can't manage people effectively.

Privacy Please

Unlike praise which may be given both in private and in public, criticism to an individual should never be given in public. Individual criticism delivered in the presence of an employee's peers diminishes the employee's dignity, and people need dignity to perform effectively. People need dignity to perform with power. This reminder about giving criticism in private, by the way, goes double for criticism intended for your boss.

I'll always remember one, gray winter afternoon. it was after 3:00 p.m. and I was already 15 minutes late for a meeting with our district managers. I entered the conference room to find eight executives glaring at me as though I had just canceled all bonuses.

Finally, Lou Elliot spoke. "Glad you could make it," he said. The room broke into laughter. "Sure is nice of you to take time out of your busy day to visit with us." He wouldn't stop. "I suppose the next time you call a meeting, you'll expect us to be on time but it'll be okey-dokey if you come in whenever." There was more laughter but, this time, I could sense a certain discomfort in the room and thought perhaps some managers believed he was taking things too far.

"Alright, alright," I said, "I'm very sorry. I got caught up on the telephone and I just plain forgot about this meeting. I apologize to you all. Now, let's get started, shall we?" With that, I called the meeting to order and began covering some of the things on my mind. "First, let's run through that list of changes in our ordering policies. We can start with . . ."

"Hold it, hold your horses!" It was Lou again.

"Yes, Lou. What is it?"

"This is not the first time you've kept us waiting. I think you owe us more than a brief apology. I think you ought to guarantee you'll value our time just as you expect us to value yours."

I could feel the hair on my neck rising. What's with this guy, I thought. I apologized, didn't I? What's he want, and does he think he's speaking for everyone? I felt cornered. So, he has a point, I thought, so what? I can't let him have at me like this. If I lose control here, I'll lose my ability to control other situations.

I've always encouraged managers to debate with me and challenge my ideas as long as the discussion was confined to the issues. I believe in spirited, rational arguing. I think it is healthy in an organization. The only way to get beneath the surface of an idea is to rub it against the sandpaper of criticism. The coarser the sandpaper, the deeper you can get beneath the surface and the more you can see what the idea is made of.

Suddenly, I realized that my problem with Lou Elliot just might have stemmed from the fact that our employees have always had the freedom to argue with me. But this was different; this was personal. This wasn't criticism of an idea, this was criticism of me—in public.

I knew I had to put an end to this, and now, or it could get out of hand. I spoke firmly, emphatically. I wanted no doubt I meant business. "I'll tell you what, Lou. If you want to discuss this with me, you may do so after this meeting, in private. Right now, we're going to continue."

Lou was stunned. "But, you can't cut me off . . ."

"Listen up," I said. "We will not discuss this here. I'm firm about that. We can discuss this in private, later, but not here. Am I making myself clear, Lou? Right now, we're going on with this meeting. You may leave if you can't do that."

There was a long, silent pause and I started the meeting again. It was an uncomfortable moment, especially for Lou, but before long, the discussion resumed its usual brisk vitality. Lou didn't contribute for a while. But, by meeting's end, he was participating in a typically energetic way.

Criticism at its best is a tool for improving performance, but it is only effective when used correctly. Criticism should be delivered directly to the source of the problem with clarity and specificity about changes required. It may be O.K. to criticize your boss—that depends on your boss—but never do it in public. For that matter, never criticize anyone in public, including those who report to you. Criticism given in private protects the dignity of the person being criticized, and people need dignity to perform effectively and with power.

The Sandwich Treatment

Realizing how sensitive people can be when receiving criticism, I employed what I called "The Sandwich Treatment." It was such an effective device for giving criticism, I encouraged all of our top managers to use it.

The Sandwich Treatment is a package. Criticism, including appropriate constructive suggestions, is sandwiched between two big slices of praise. It's not contrived. Rather, it's intended to discourage the employee from blowing the criticism out of proportion. It helps put the criticism in perspective.

I would begin by telling the employee of his or her finest qualities and best performance characteristics. Then, I'd gently give the criticism together with detailed specifics about what I wanted changed. I'd try to do that with extreme clarity so nothing would be misunderstood. When the changes I wanted were extensive or complicated, I'd have them typed out beforehand so I could literally hand them to the employee.

When I finished giving the criticism, I'd complete the sandwich by reinforcing the original message that the employee was valued, was not in danger of losing his or her job, and was expected to be around for a long time to come. I emphasized that I, personally, hoped that would be true.

And finally, after I'd given The Sandwich Treatment, the praise-criticism-praise package, as authors Kenneth Blanchard and Spencer Johnson articulate in their best seller, *The One Minute Manager*, I'd try to catch the employee in the act of doing things right so I could praise his or her behavior and reinforce the changes I wanted. And, as the authors suggest, the sooner this praise is given, the better. Positive reinforcement is always most effective when it is given immediately following the criticism or as soon after as possible.

* * *

Summary

1. When receiving criticism, avoid being defensive. Keep thinking.

2. Trust that you are valuable to your company and see the criticism as information you need to perform more satisfactorily for your boss.

3. When giving criticism, don't merely describe what's wrong. Provide instruction on how to solve the problem and do things better.

4. Praise may be given in public, but always give criticism in private.

5. To put criticism in perspective, try "sandwiching" the criticism between two big slices of praise.

Chapter 14

Getting the Boss to
Notice You

We know what happens to people who stay in the middle of the road. They get run over.

—Aneurin Bevan

Getting noticed by the boss isn't automatic. Even good bosses get so involved in their own professional and private lives at times that having time to notice the accomplishments of every employee becomes all but impossible. Sometimes, the pressure of work can make a boss nearsighted and, unfortunately, when bosses become myopic, they can behave downright badly. Many years ago, I had a boss like that.

I was 23. I had just finished my bachelor's degree and wasn't ready to think about graduate school. I needed a job. I looked for a job for nine solid weeks and finally landed a spot as a junior salesman in the new car division of a Chevrolet dealership.

"All right people, here's what's up." Our sales manager had just started the Monday morning meeting. He stood facing us at the front of the room with a paper cup of steaming coffee in one hand and a used, unlit cigar in the other. I remember thinking the only thing he was missing was a big, colorful, windowpane plaid jacket.

"We're competing in a national contest for the month of September," he continued, "and the dealership that sells the most this month will win a big—I mean a BIG—prize."

He had the disgusting habit of chewing on the end of that dead cigar after every agenda item as if to add emphasis. I was excited nevertheless. Finally out of school, I was an adult at last, making my own way and now I had a chance to win a terrific prize. I couldn't wait to hear what it was.

"If we win," he went on, "my wife and I will get an all-expenses-paid trip to Bermuda. That's Bermuda, in the Caribbean," he emphasized. "We've never been to Bermuda, and this is our one big chance. So I want you people to pull out all the stops! Put in the time! Call those cards! We're going to win in September!"

I couldn't believe my ears. I was burning mad. I had trouble controlling myself and blurted out, "Is that it?"

He turned and said, "Wha d'ya mean, 'Is that it'?"

"Well," I replied, "I don't understand why we should work real hard just so you can go to Bermuda." I believed I was speaking for everyone, "What do we get if we win the contest?"

Obviously irritated, he glared at me. "Look, kid, you're new here, aren't you? When you've been around a while, you can ask all the questions you want. Anybody else?" he demanded. No one spoke. The meeting was over.

I was fuming. As we filed out, a seasoned veteran took my elbow and pulled me aside. He told me the best thing I could do was to relax and have a little patience. "Most of the contests in this place," he explained, "are really designed for the sales people, and most of the prizes are won by sales people. This guy is generally pretty good," he added. "I suggest you just take a deep breath and let it pass."

"But he was . . . ," I mumbled. "We don't . . . This isn't . . ."

"Take it easy kid," he said. "You'll see. It'll work out."

Sure enough, a few days later the sales manger called another meeting to announce that if our dealership won the trip to Bermuda, it would go to the sales person who had the best overall performance. He also had the courage and, as I think back on it, the class to apologize publicly for losing his cool.

I understood. He really was O.K. Winter was coming and he just got all caught up in the possibility of an all-expenses-paid trip to Bermuda. Bosses suffer from egocentrism too.

The point is employees need to recognize that bosses are subject to the same streams of thoughts and pressures as employees. Bosses have good days, bad days, problems at work, children to raise, bills to pay and dreams to pursue. In other words, just like employees, bosses have dozens of things in their professional and personal lives begging for their attention.

As president of our company, I'd be concerned about a variety of things on a typical business day: increasing sales in the southwest, preparing for an upcoming board meeting, installing three new retail stores in Florida, and getting ready for a meeting with our tax accountants. And, on any given day, I was also concerned with my personal matters. I might have had a birthday party to plan, a speech to prepare for a week from Thursday, a report from my physician concerning my cholesterol level. I might even have had an argument with my wife.

I realized that every staff member, every employee, brought his or her own personal world into the office. For example, our vice president of administration might be worrying about the merits of a new computer system, remodeling the shipping line and implementing a revision in our customer returns policy, taking his dog to the vet, scheduling his car for a tuneup, and purchasing a gift for his wife to celebrate their anniversary. Our sales director might have been concerned about firing the new salesperson, instituting a new sales report system, developing a promotion campaign, an impending visit from his in-laws, his father's recent heart attack, and attending the Boy Scout Jamboree with his son next weekend.

And so it is in any organization—hundreds, maybe thousands of separate lives come together, each with a unique and long list of individual goals, problems and priorities. Like employees, bosses also live busy lives. Knowing this should help one understand how bosses can sometimes overlook or miss completely the best achievements of their employees. That's why solid performers are sometimes overlooked.

You Gotta Sell Yourself

With so many issues competing for the boss's attention in every business day, it's easy—not desirable, but easy—to take the steady performers for granted and just focus on the matters screaming for attention. It's hard to hear anything when there's so much noise. And, too often in these busy circumstances, when bosses finally do become aware of the stellar performance and exceptional achievements of an employee, it's simpler to just take comfort in the fact that the employee is performing well and not make the effort to translate that exceptional performance into a bid by the employee for a promotion.

It's not enough for a good employee to have something to offer, the boss has to know what it is you've got. If the boss doesn't recognize your value, your special qualities won't do you any good. So, you can't just do your job and hope your boss will trip over your potential. You cannot sit back and wait to be discovered. You can't assume that it will happen by itself, because it rarely does. It's your responsibility, no one else's, to bring your accomplishments, your talent, your skills and your potential for more responsibility to the boss's attention. You have to take the bull by its horns and make things happen. You have to be able to sell yourself.

It doesn't matter whether you're selling a product or an idea; if you want to be successful you've got to find your customer's hot buttons, the triggers which fire the motivation to buy. We all have hot buttons. When pushed, they enable us to say the words every salesperson hungers for: "Yes, I want what you're selling; I'm ready to buy; where do I sign?"

Unfortunately for many salespeople, most customers' hot buttons are rarely on the surface. They are hard to find and are usually surrounded by a wall of defenses. Every buyer has these defenses. Like a coat of armor, each of us carries around a built-in defense mechanism which keeps us from acting on impulse and protects us from being "sold." It makes us rethink the purchase and question our motives for buying. "Do I need it? Can I afford it? How will I pay for it? Will it last? What guarantees are there? Is there a better alternative? What is the downside? Should I wait a while?"

The real problem for sellers is that most buyers won't explain all their reasons for not buying. Sure, they'll freely discuss the obvious advantages and disadvantages of what you're selling. They'll ask questions about performance and service, and they love to compare the pros and cons of your arguments with those of your competition, but they often keep their most personal feelings to themselves. They are usually reluctant to talk about their ability to afford what you're selling, and they may hide their fears about making a mistake, or about what their neighbors or colleagues may think, or about how their bosses or boards will react.

These are the hidden agendas most buyers bring to their conversations with salespeople. These are their personal and private issues which can turn a sale or destroy it. These are the heart and soul of why buyers buy, hidden from view and safeguarded by a barrier of natural defenses. These are their hot buttons.

Some salespeople mistakenly believe that selling intensity will break down this buyer resistance. They pound on the surface with an onslaught of words and random arguments hoping this blitzkrieg will penetrate the buyer's defenses. Admittedly, with luck and sheer persistence, they sometimes succeed. But, more often than not, this blind thrashing about fails to get them through the buyer's armor and they miss making the sale.

The most effective sales people well understand that when the customer is engaged in a conversation with the salesperson, it is because he or she wants to buy. But they also know that before they can make the sale they must learn exactly what the customer wants. It is no different when you want to sell yourself or even an idea to your boss. Before you can hit your boss's hot buttons, you've got to get through his defenses and identify the issues important to him. Often, he'll tell you what they are, but you've got to answer his questions and resolve his reservations—even when he doesn't verbalize them. Without doing so, you have almost no chance of making the sale.

How to Push Your Boss's Buttons

It helps to know that all bosses have in common certain things. They all have jobs to do, goals to reach and problems to solve. And, not unlike employees, they all have circumstances in their lives or situations in their companies which complicate their jobs and limit their ability to get things done. In other words, they all have things which get in their way and make their jobs more difficult to do, or take longer, or cost more.

While your boss may have other issues which affect the outcome of your selling effort, it is almost certain he has these. It follows that selling the boss will be easier and more successful if these issues, those the boss cares about, are addressed. It's called benefit selling, which simply means you spend less time and energy describing what you are selling and more describing what it will do for the customer.

An advertising genius once commented, "We don't sell the steak, we sell the sizzle." In the same vein, if you're selling light bulbs, don't describe the light bulb. Rather, explain what the light bulb will do for the customer. Forget about what it looks like and how the filament works. Explain how it will make it easier to see at night. Explain that electric light is cheaper and safer than kerosene lamps. Sell the benefits. Don't sell the bulb; sell the light.

I had minor surgery a few years ago, and I'll never forget the doctor's explanation of what was going to happen. He came into the office where I had been waiting and sat down across from me. He was dressed in casual tan slacks and a navy blue blazer with antiqued brass buttons. Except for the stethoscope which dangled in front of his tie, he could have been on his way to a garden party or, I thought, perhaps he had just come from golf.

"This is going to be quick and easy," he said. "The nurse will get you ready and wind things up afterwards. I'll come in and do the actual surgery, of course, but that will only take about 20 minutes. It used to take three hours to do one of these, but now, we've really got a system." He smiled with pride. "We do 30 or 40 procedures a day." Then, knowing I ran a business, he spoke in what he thought was my language. "You understand," he said with a knowing wink, "it helps the bottom line."

Well, of course I understood. With my eyes closed I could appreciate that a system which speeded up his office routine and got his patients in and out with assembly line efficiency would make surgery— my surgery—more profitable for this effete social butterfly. But at that moment I wasn't interested in his "business." I was going to have surgery and all I wanted to know was what this surgery meant for me. After all, I was the customer, wasn't I? Couldn't he have understood my issues, my concerns? Wouldn't it have been easy enough to translate the attributes of the surgical procedure in terms appropriate to me?

Suppose he had said something like this: "This is going to be quick and easy, you'll see. The nurse will get you ready and then I'll come in and do the surgery. It's really a very simple procedure and quite common, and with modern techniques and today's technology it will only take 20 minutes, tops. It will be over before you realize it and you'll hardly feel a thing. And afterward, if you like, I'll give you my home phone number so you can call me if you have any questions at all."

Ideal? Maybe. But a good bedside manner is something we could all use when relating to others. It's really nothing more than taking care of the other person's feelings. It's tuning in to the other person's needs and behaving in ways that take them into account. It's a lot like benefit selling, which means you spend less time on you and more on the customer. It's selling with a focus on what the customer wants and needs. Can you think of a better way to make the sale?

Harry had been quiet for some time. I wasn't sure I was being clear enough about specifically what he had to do to get noticed. "What it comes down to is this, Harry," I explained. "You've got to be able to sell yourself."

He cleared his throat, "I hate the idea of selling. It seems so . . . well, so pushy. If I'm doing all the right things, I'd like to think my boss would see my potential without my having to sell it to him."

"There is a myth about selling, Harry," I said, "and I want to dispel it right now. The myth is this: A good product will sell itself. Now, there's an element of truth in that, of course. It always pays to have a good product, but even good products have to be sold. Sales don't happen by themselves. Someone has to communicate with the buyer.

"There's another myth, too. It is that good selling involves a lot of fast talking."

"You got that right," he said.

"The fact is nothing could be further from the truth," I replied. "The best selling has nothing to do with fast talking. It's related to meeting needs. It's understanding what the customer wants, making sure you have what the customer wants, and communicating that fact effectively. It's not fast talking, Harry. It's saying the right things."

"But selling is . . . well, it just doesn't' feel right."

"There's nothing wrong with selling," I said. "Everybody sells."

"Everybody," he echoed. "You mean like sideshow barkers and dope peddlers?"

"Even hookers, Harry," I said smiling. "Everybody sells. From General Motors to I.B.M., from the federal government to the March of Dimes, everybody sells. Parents, teachers, priests, ministers, rabbis, doctors, lawyers, accountants, architects—everybody sells. Universities, hospitals, banks, the Smithsonian Institution, The Department of Agriculture, the Secretary of State, the President, even the Pope—everybody sells.

"And you, Harry, you're no different. If you want to get your message across, you've got to be willing to sell it. It would be nice to think your boss is out there looking for all the good things you do, but that's wishful thinking. That's dreaming. Your boss is busy with lots of things. There's too much to do, too much noise. Now, that may not be a good excuse, but that's the way it is. You've got to see that reality and take charge for your own sake. You've got to be willing to make your own case."

"It ought to be a two-way street," he said. "I understand what you're saying about not waiting for good things to happen, but selling yourself is a tall order. We need better communication."

"You're right, Harry. We do need better communication. Employees and their bosses ought to talk to one another. It would help them both. Bosses should explain more clearly what it is they expect from the people who report to them, but don't lose sight of the fact that it doesn't always happen the way it should. Employees have to be willing to ask what's expected of them, just like you did when you first came in here. Then we can have a dialogue like we're having now."

"Sure, we're talking now," he agreed. "But this isn't typical. This isn't the way it normally is. What usually happens is the boss makes the rules and decides everything else about the job and the employee is expected to follow orders. That's the way it usually is."

I wanted to emphasize that many bosses are available to talk to their employees, one-on-one, by Harry wouldn't let me get started.

"So what we're doing now," he said, "talking like this, is not typical in this company."

"I have to admit, Harry, what we're doing now is not normal day-in and day-out communication. While a back-and-forth discussion is fine after hours, it's usually not possible during the work day. There's too much to do. And besides, the fact is, this isn't a democracy."

His eyes widened and he looked at me directly. "You're telling me!"

I went on. "It can't be a democracy, Harry. Bosses give directions and employees have to follow them. That's the only way a company can function, the only way an organization can perform effectively. Without absolute clarity about who's in charge, we'd all be going in different directions, we'd be working at cross purposes. In any company, or even within a department in the company, there has to be someone at the top calling signals."

"I understand that," Harry said.

"In addition to signal callers, we need people who can be team players," I continued. "Hopefully, as time goes on, some of those people will develop into leaders. We can always use more good leaders in this company."

"Well, you could do something about that right now, if you wanted to," he noted. "I can tell you this: a lot of people here would like to have more responsibility."

"And, I'd like to give them more, Harry. After all, I need all the help I can get. But first, I want to see evidence the employee is ready for a promotion. I have to know in advance that he or she is capable of shouldering more responsibility. Most bosses do. They want to know an employee will be successful in the new position."

"How can bosses know that in advance?" Harry asked. "Nobody has a crystal ball."

"There are a number of ways," I said.

How to Demonstrate Your Potential

Bosses are impressed by employees who show they've got what it takes. They can do that by taking charge of the issues around them and tackling them as though they know they can come up with solutions. Nothing turns bosses on more than employees who don't need to be told what to do.

Harry wanted to stop and make sure he understood where this was going. "O.K.," he said, "bosses like employees who go about solving problems and do it with optimism, people who tackle problems believing they will find solutions. Is that right?"

"Yes, the way they go about it is important. And, they don't come to their bosses with every little problem expecting the boss to hand them a solution. When they recognize a problem, they take it on as if it was theirs to solve—not their boss's. If information is needed, they go after it. No one tells them they should go after more information, they just go get it. If a policy needs revision, they think the problem through and come up with a recommendation on how to revise the policy. If other people need to be involved, they talk to those people and try to get them involved. And they do it without waiting for the boss to hand them a recipe, a manual with instructions on how to go about it."

"And that's what turns bosses on, the initiative, is that what you're saying?"

"Yes. Bosses turn on to that because the people they promote must have initiative. But more important, the boss wants to see it before a promotion is given. You remember my saying that I want evidence an employee is ready for a promotion beforehand. I want to know in advance the employee will be successful in a new position. What better case could I make for finding ways to demonstrate leadership potential?

"The hard truth is this," I continued. "It's impossible for an employee to demonstrate management potential without acting like a manager. Waiting around for somebody with a magic wand to make a pronouncement that permission has been granted to do things won't do it."

Harry sat down, and in a voice softer than before, he said, "I'm beginning to get the picture."

Some employees watch the clock, waiting for five o'clock when they can breathe that great sigh of relief which says, "It's over. I am finally finished for the day and now I can put this #*/&%#@*! job behind me and get back to my life."

These employees appear to have separated their existence into two, independent, almost mutually exclusive halves. The first half is their personal life, their have-fun, be-yourself, take-no-orders-from-anyone, "private" life. The second half, and I do mean second, is the always serious, full-of-pressure, I-have-no-choice-in-the-matter, working life. It's "where I have to go each day." It's "the plant," "the office," "the job." Somewhere, somehow, they got the idea that enjoying one's life and work are two totally separate things—two completely incompatible entities. They have decided that one is enjoyable; the other is not.

These employees don't enjoy their jobs. They come to work because they need to earn a living. There's nothing wrong with that, of course, we all have to earn a living, but earning a livelihood should not be the only reason we work. We need other things in our lives. We need the companionship of other human beings. We need to be challenged, we need to feel a sense of accomplishment, and we need recognition. We all need these things and no place are they more available than on the job. So, why don't more people enjoy and benefit from these virtues of work?

It may be that the boss is not effective in creating an environment where employees can appreciate these things. Yes, some bosses are lousy managers; some can't constructively challenge employees and have limited skills giving recognition. But, very often, that is not the answer. Too frequently, it's just an excuse. I have seen so many people come to brand new jobs already convinced that work is a necessary evil, I can only conclude that some people can't see any other possibility. With this mind set, how could they begin to recognize a healthy work environment even where one exists? Opportunities for enjoying work are lost to these employees because they are blind to them from the beginning.

There is only one way to make sure you are not making the same mistake, only one way to give yourself what you deserve—the chance to like your work. Give your company, your boss and your job the benefit of the doubt. It's that simple. Give yourself the option to enjoy working. Allow your job to be part of your life—your entire life—your private life, too. Integrate it into your whole existence.

Now, I don't mean to suggest the way to get ahead is to become a workaholic. I am not proposing that you could make a daily habit of bringing your work home with you. Your family life, your "private" life is important too. And, like everyone, you've got to have time away from work to rest and recuperate. You need distance from work to recharge your batteries.

But, in order to get to the place where you can enjoy the challenges, the people, the environment of working, it's got to be O.K. with you to take your work home now and then. You can't confine your work to a nine-to-five daytime compartment—at least, not if you expect to win significant promotions. You've got be willing to take it home when it's necessary, come in early or stay late when that's what it takes to meet a deadline. You've got to be willing to think about your work anytime, in the morning, at dinner and when you go to sleep.

Your work has to be part of your life—your whole life—not just the hours when you're in the office. It's got to be O.K. with you to think about yourself, at least partly, in terms of your work. It's got be part of who you are.

These are the people bosses look for when they've got a big job to do. They want people willing to be involved in their work from their toes to the tips of their fingers. They want people who get up in the morning chaffing at the bit, anxious to come to work because they've got things to do and goals to accomplish. In short, they want people who want more than "a job." They want people who like to work.

The Right Way to Ask for a Raise

The direct approach is the simplest and most effective way to put your case squarely before the boss.

The best example of the direct approach I ever had the occasion to witness occurred in the autumn of 1975. Andrea Stevens, a young woman who had worked for our company for about three years, asked to see me one morning about something she described as, "A matter of great importance to her, to me and the company."

I was intrigued. What could it be, I wondered, that would be of great importance to her, the company and me? She had me hooked.

I had a very full schedule that day, so I made an appointment to see her at the end of the afternoon. Several times during that day I found myself wondering what Andrea Stevens was going to tell me. She worked in our bookkeeping department and because she reported to a level of management two levels below mine, I hadn't the opportunity to get to know her very well. I was curious. Who was this gutsy young woman and what did she have to tell me?

On schedule, she came into my office, shook my hand firmly and said with confidence, "I'm glad you could see me. I know you are busy and I'd like to come straight to the point."

I loved it! How could she have had the foresight to know that my days were filled with consultants, salespeople, customers and employees, most of whom had difficulty coming to the point; most of whom made an arduous practice of beating around the bush in the hopes of strengthening and justifying whatever arguments they were making? Some lacked a clear point from beginning to end. Some were perfectionists who took pains to qualify every word. Here was an employee who wanted to come straight to the point. I told her, "Please go on."

"I came to you because I want you to know I am ready for more work and more responsibility." She said, "I have both the talent and the capacity for more." And then she concluded with the clincher: "And I am ready," she emphasized READY, "for a new and bigger challenge."

There it was, all wrapped up in three short sentences. Clean, direct and definitely to the point. She said, "I'm talented, I'm capable of taking on more responsibility," and, "I'm ready for a new challenge." What she didn't say was just as important as what she did say. She didn't say, "I want more money."

Certainly she wanted more money. I knew that. Everybody wants to make more money, and most of the time you don't have to spell that out for the boss. It goes without saying.

The point here is that, without the words, Andrea did ask for money, but she asked in the boss's language—in a way that emphasized she was willing to work for it. She said she was capable of assuming greater responsibility and willing to put in more time, energy, talent and effort to increase her value to me by contributing more to the company. What she said clearly and in capital letters was: "Let me do more. I'm capable of doing more. I want to do more." She didn't' say, "I want more money." She said, "I'm capable of earning more money!" I understood her immediately.

Andrea Stevens said it differently than the majority of employees say it. She said, "I want an opportunity to *earn* more money," and she said it in a way that was not only totally refreshing but extremely powerful.

The next day, I met with her supervisor and I shared the essence of our brief conversation. I suggested Andrea Stevens be given an opportunity to take on some new tasks and that her responsibilities should be enlarged as soon as she proved capable of handling them. Finally, I asked to be informed of her progress so I could personally congratulate her along the way and make sure each addition to her workload was accompanied by a bump in salary.

Month by month she took on more, growing steadlily in her capacity to handle new responsibilities and contribute to the progress of our company. She worked longer hours and took work home as necessary. At meetings she was always prepared and her comments were always on the point.

Like all of us, she made mistakes along the way. But when she made mistakes, she always owned up to them personally, and never let the blame for errors made under her direction fall to the people who reported to her. Frequently, she directed my attention to the achievements of employees whom she supervised and encouraged me to recognize them and even promote them when she thought it would benefit the company. She credited others for good ideas and never took credit that wasn't hers. On the other hand, she worked hard to keep me informed of her achievement and didn't hide from recognition when it was earned.

Andrea Stevens was with me 10 years in all. In that time she grew to become a vice president. Needless to say, she had the talent to make a significant contribution to our company and, in so doing, she added spectacular impetus to her own professional advancement and financial prosperity.

Yet, without a willingness to take on more work and assume greater responsibility, without the capacity to change her perspective and see things from my point of view, and without the courage to bring herself to my attention, she might not have advanced at all.

"How about you, Harry?" I asked. "Why don't you grab a piece of the action? It's there for you. Start looking for things we could do better and, when you find them, don't wait to sink your teeth into them. Take the initiative, Harry. Begin right now to see that's what your boss really wants."

*   *   *

Summary

1. Keep all verbal and written communication brief and to the point. Send copies of your memos to appropriate others so they will know what you are doing.
2. Take yourself seriously so others will. Always speak positively about yourself, your responsibilities and the company.
3. Take part in company fund drives, outings and other activities. Do some community volunteer work.
4. Get to know the managers above you.
5. Keep a journal of your projects and activities so you are always prepared to review your contributions and accomplishments.
6. Walk with purpose, as if you're always involved, energetic and busy.
7. Be straight with your boss. If you are capable of doing more, ask for it.

Chapter 15

What If Your Boss Is a Dud

If you wish the world to advance; your merits you're bound to enhance. You must stir it up and stump it, and blow your own trumpet—or trust me, you haven't a chance.

—William S. Gilbert

Suppose your direct supervisor, your boss, your conduit to the top is a loser. Let's say you've recently come on board and it didn't take you long to recognize that fact. How are you going to deal with the problem and have any hope of getting ahead? Here's a case in point.

Kristin Burns was hired by a large general hospital as director of industrial marketing services, which meant she had primary responsibility for packaging hospital services and selling them to self-insured corporations, HMO's and other health plans. She reported directly to the vice president of marketing, Michael Carlson.

Carlson was a lifer. He'd been at the hospital almost 25 years. Kristin thought that he had probably done a dynamite job at one time, which would account for his being a vice president, but his retirement was just a few years down that road, and now he seemed to be marking time. She could see that, for the most part, he was not focusing on producing. He was strictly nine-to-five. He spent hours reviewing trade journals and the daily paper. Often, the door to his office was closed—he said he was "in conference." Summer meant two-hour lunches on the tennis court, and winter, mid-afternoons at the club.

He didn't initiate new projects and, worse, all of Kristin's best ideas seemed to die at his office door. He pigeon-holed her suggestions and never brought them to the attention of the hospital's president or other executives. Actually, he avoided meetings with the president and other VP's unless he had no other choice.

Kristin could easily have vented her frustration to co-workers and others, or even gone directly to the hospital president, but she feared a crusade against Carlson might backfire. She was uncertain as to why he was still on the payroll and she didn't yet know what his relationship with the president was—not an uncommon situation for new employees with weak bosses. She heard rumors the president was aware that Carlson was a weak link, but still, she couldn't understand why nobody had dealt with the problem.

As time went on, Kristin noted that co-workers and other executives were courteous and respectful of her boss but, generally, maneuvered around him. He was rarely included in top level decisions and it became increasingly clear the people on the top were ignoring him hoping the problem would just go away. She saw a kind of group denial working, an attitude that said, "leave well enough alone." It was like having an elephant in your living room. Everyone knew it was there, but nobody talked about it. This was a system, she decided, that was not used to dealing with issues head on. Some corporate cultures are like that. Fortunately, all are not.

Kristin was unusually intuitive and extremely sensitive to the environment around her. She could "feel" that a move to another level for input and guidance might not have been acceptable, especially because she was a relative newcomer. Yet, while she saw there were definite opportunities for growth at the hospital, she knew they were limited as long as she remained closeted inside her boss's department.

She understood that doing anything to circumvent her boss was risky but she felt she had to do something and was willing to face the consequences if she failed. She knew, in order to preserve any hope of getting promoted, she would have to perform effectively in her current job and, somehow, find a way to bring herself to the attention of her boss's boss. In order to do that, she devised a strategy—a survival plan. The goal was to manage the current situation in a way which ensured her boss would not inhibit her ability and desire to be productive.

Kristin's Strategy for Flourishing in Spite of a Bad Boss

1. Maintain regular contact with the boss but stop looking for direction and approval.
2. Set your own agenda, make your own decisions and keep track of all activities, meetings and accomplishments.
3. Schedule your own meetings with other executives but always inform your boss when a meeting is scheduled and invite his or her attendance.
4. Inform the boss of every move, involving him or her in discussions and in the process whenever possible.
5. Be assertive when it matters but, always, remain as non-threatening as possible.
6. Keep frustrations and negative thoughts to yourself and absolutely avoid bad-mouthing the boss in any way, to anyone, including your best friend at work.
7. Always treat the boss with respect, both in the boss's presence and in the presence of others.

Some people are going to shout, "It's too phony, I just can't do it! The boss is the dead weight, not me. Why should I have to screw around with this?" My only response is it's the most practical thing to do. It's self-preservation. It's a way to take charge of a bad situation and make it work for you.

Kristin followed her strategy to the letter. She presented ideas in a way that made her boss part of the process. She never met with anyone on a business related matter without making sure he knew about the meeting ahead of time and had been invited to join her. After meetings, whether he attended them or not, she gave him full, written reports as to what was discussed and what decisions were made.

Kristin's strategy was clean. She would not let her boss keep her from performing to the best of her ability. She would focus all of her energy on her performance, lousy boss or not. She was prepared to handle the situation the best she could and reassured herself that, no matter how green the grass looked across the fence, no job is perfect.

She wasn't willing to risk going to the president to complain about her boss and she didn't waste time or energy wrestling with why the president didn't act. Instead, she accepted the possibility there was a good reason her boss was still there. "If the president is bright enough to be president and I do things to make myself visible," she decided, "sooner or later I'll be seen." So, she turned the spotlight on herself and put energy into improving her own performance.

Kristin believed that people are pretty smart. She was right. Most bosses know what's going on even though it sometimes appears they don't. Most of the time they know who's making things happen and who isn't.

Given that Kristin saw opportunities for growth at the hospital, the decision to find a way to be effective in spite of her boss was a good first strategy. She knew she needed to give it time. She also knew if she was unsuccessful in making an impression which would catapult her into another department, she could then begin to look for another job. She didn't want to develop a record for jumping from one job to another, so, for the time being, she decided to give this job a legitimate chance.

As president, I've seen this predicament from the other side. Over the years, I've had a number of middle level managers who were great at many things but poor at getting the most from people who reported to them. It was frustrating. Their employees, bright people, could not understand why I didn't just get rid of these managers. They must have thought I was asleep at the wheel or, perhaps, they thought there was more there than a normal boss-employee relationship. This experience helped me understand how employees come to believe it's not what you know, but who you know that counts. In reality, both count.

Often, these managers contributed in ways not immediately apparent to their employees and replacing them was not always an easy thing. I also admit to procrastinating. I hated the prospect of firing anyone, especially someone who had come up through the ranks and given us a lot of good years. It was hard to face the fact that our company was outgrowing the abilities of some of our long term managers and I always found myself thinking twice and three times and four times about terminating any one of them. I agonized over those situations and, as a result, postponed acting, no doubt to the anguish of some employees and the detriment of our company.

The circumstances I'm describing are probably not unlike the one in Kristin's hospital. Kristin couldn't know for sure what the hospital's president was thinking yet she gave him the benefit of the doubt. She was flexible, willing to change and adapt. Her decision to hang in there and give her a job a legitimate chance to succeed paid off. In time, her boss was forced into early retirement and she was made marketing director. A couple of years later, she was promoted to vice president.

Increasing Your Visibility

While Kristin was correct believing most bosses know who's making things happen and who isn't—it helps to make sure they do. We often take our boss and our boss's boss for granted but the smart employee keeps them informed. One very effective way is to write regular memos reminding them that you are a producer and, therefore, capable and ready to assume a bigger job and greater responsibility. Of course, they'll want to know how well you're doing in your current job. Tell them. Put your projects on paper in a concise, easy-to-read report. Let them know what you're up to. Let them know what you're accomplishing. Remember, if you want to be promoted, you've got to be visible. The "boss" has to know you're there.

"Sure," you say, "I'd write memos, but my boss and his boss already know what I'm doing. If I write a memo, they might think I'm wasting time, writing memos about problems with time that would be better spent working on them. Anyway, I hate playing politics."

The people I'm talking about are busy and you are not the only employee they think about. You have a good deal of competition for the boss's attention simply because there are other employees vying for his time. If you don't want to be lost in the blur of people who report to him, you've got to find ways to stand out. If it's well done, writing a memo or report is an excellent way to increase your visibility. The idea is to give your boss peace of mind about you and what you're doing and let him know you're ready for bigger things.

Most employees communicate with their bosses only when they have problems. While that's always important, it's also worthwhile to let your boss know when things are going well. So few of the employees who reported to me did this, I was always very impressed by those who did. It made me stop and think about that employee to better understand what he or she was doing. It made me focus on the kinds of problems being handled and assess how well the employee was handling them. It made me appreciate and remember the employee.

Let me add a word of caution. Sitting down to write a report off the top of your head can be dangerous. Memos and reports full of fluff will damage your image. Your reports must be worth reading. They should provide information the boss needs. Take time to prepare. Think about your job and the things you are working on. What do you know that your boss might want to know? Can you tell him something that will enable him to avoid a problem or make things run more smoothly? Can you provide information that will make his job easier?

Remember, the boss likes good news too. List activities that let him know there is progress toward a goal and identify the goals achieved. Don't forget other people's achievements. If you're impressed with the performance of folks that report to you, tell your boss, and tell him in writing. Then, send a copy of your memo to the employee. What a wonderful way to create a sense of good will and teamwork. It will enhance loyalty on the part of your employee and, I assure you, it will impress your boss.

Your report can be as simple as a one-page document which pulls together loose ends and clarifies existing information. For example, a receptionist could summarize on paper how different people in the company want their phones answered. The purpose in creating such a memo would be to have it available for substitute receptionists when she is on vacation or ill.

But the smart receptionist wouldn't stop there. She would circulate the memo among the firm's executives for verification that she has correctly recorded their preferences. In doing so, she would demonstrate in unmistakable terms that her work is important to her, she puts energy into thinking about her department and the potential problems within it and, most important, is capable of creating solutions.

The variety of material which can be organized into a useful report is endless in almost any job. Sales people can create charts of decision makers and gate keepers at the businesses on which they call. Retail sales clerks can take notice of customer reaction to new displays and summarize them for their managers. Secretaries and bookkeepers can prepare road maps to their filing systems so others can use them when necessary. Telemarketers can summarize objections and compile their most successful answers. Data processing people can create a dictionary of terms, customer service people can summarize the most frequently asked questions and telephone order clerks can track complaints and describe a solution. Department managers and supervisors, nurses, cooks, desk clerks, truck drivers, cashiers, security, maintenance and delivery people—almost anyone—can summarize the nuances, the little things about their jobs they only get to know when they've been at them a while.

Producing a meaningful report is easiest if you have something from which to work. Keep a log. Note with whom you meet, what you talk about, the problems you are working on and what you've accomplished. And, by all means, deliver your report in writing. Oral reports are acceptable when immediate feedback is needed or when your boss requests one. Written reports are preferred, however, because they can be reviewed at your boss's convenience and show you have respect for his or her time.

Part of a great strategy to get promoted is keeping your name in front of the people who count. Carefully considered, well written memos create opportunities for further communication, which is the cornerstone of high visibility.

But, when none of this works, when you've performed well and made yourself visible, when you've demonstrated your ability and communicated your willingness to assume greater responsibility, when you've done all this and still received no signal that your talent is recognized—it may be time to talk to your boss's boss.

When to Talk to Your Boss's Boss

Make no mistake about it, going over your boss's head is risky business. It can get you fired. The only time, therefore, to talk to your boss's boss is after you've talked to your boss—after you've talked to your boss and gotten nowhere. Let me say it again: Don't ever go to your boss's boss with a complaint about your boss until you've first had a chance to talk to your boss and given him or her adequate time to respond to the problem. Why should you talk to your boss when you know he is unresponsive, territorial and unreasonable? Because, and I guarantee it, the first question our boss's boss is going to ask is: "Have your talked to your boss about this?"

Very few employees came immediately to me when they felt stagnated by their bosses. I discouraged it. When they did, I sent them straight back to their bosses with advice they work things out. Every organization must have a chain of command, if for nothing else, to divide the work. Bosses know if they undermine the authority of those who report to them, they will weaken the organization and diminish its ability to get things done.

And finally, make sure you give the situation enough time—in my opinion, about 12 months. If you run up the ladder after three months on the job, nobody will listen to you. So, before you go over your boss's head, you had better exhaust every possibility of solving the problem directly with your boss, and be certain you've given him sufficient time to do something about it.

Assuming you've talked to your boss about the problem, have been more than patient with him, and are still convinced you're on a dead-end street headed nowhere, then it may be time to talk to your boss's boss. If you're completely aware of the risks, have thoroughly weighed the consequences and made a conscious decision that, if nothing changes, you are going to look for another job, then it's time to talk to your boss's boss.

Brenda Carol is a good example of someone who knew how to talk to the boss. Brenda was an exceptionally talented woman who worked in our national training division. She knew our products and had a talent for teaching which made her extremely valuable as an installer of new franchises. She liked working for our company and understood that as long as we were growing, and we were growing rapidly, there would be opportunities for her own growth.

The training department was run by a manger who, in many ways, was an "old-timer." He had been hired just a few years after our company was founded and, almost single-handedly, put together some of the finest training programs in the industry. He was used to working alone, in his style, and when Brenda was hired, he expected her to do things his way. He wasn't looking for new ideas or new energy.

The problem was Brenda had lots of ideas, and lots of energy. On a number of occasions, she tried to share her ideas but time and again he made it clear he wasn't interested in another person's approach—especially from a "Johnny-Come-Lately," as he often referred to her. Exasperated and angry, she concluded that as long as her boss stayed in the picture her chances of getting ahead were almost nil. She would either have to make the best of a difficult situation or find another job. But before she gave up entirely, she decided she would talk to me.

Brenda did a lot of things right. When she made the appointment to see me, she reminded me that she had been with our company for almost a year and a half. She said she liked working for our company and had really wanted to stay with us for many years to come, but was now facing a situation which was forcing her to consider looking for another job. Before doing that, she said, she wanted to speak to me.

I had a pretty good idea what the meeting would be about. I had known that Brenda was a talented employee and I also knew how poor her boss's management style was. How could I not know? He reported directly to me. Of course I would see her; no boss wants to lose a good employee. I made the appointment without hesitation.

When she came into my office, she didn't waste words. She reassured me she wanted to stay but pointed out that working for her present boss was confining and frustrating. She explained she didn't take anything away from her boss's talent or the years he contributed to the company but emphasized that, unless something changed enabling her to work to her potential, she would have to look for another job.

When I asked whether she discussed this with her boss, she assured me she had. She showed me her calendar which listed all the meetings she had scheduled with her boss and pointed to notes in the margins indicating the purpose of the meetings. It was apparent from her calendar that she wanted to discuss ideas to improve the department and how she might assume more responsibility. She said none of her ideas were taken seriously. Her boss, she said, wanted things done his way and was not open to discussion, period.

She offered to share a few of her ideas to demonstrate her thinking and interest in her work. She showed me documented ways to improve efficiency in scheduling, shared outlines for six new slide presentations, and opened a file brimming with glowing letters from the accounts she had serviced.

Everything she showed me was impressive, but what was most effective about Brenda's presentation was that she helped me to see how valuable she was. It was obvious from her presentation that she had a lot to offer, and she made it clear, not with words, but with evidence, that we would be foolish to allow her to take all that talent to a competitor.

The ball was in my court. I had to find a way to keep from losing Brenda. I now knew I had a great deal to lose if her situation wasn't improved. The problem with the old-timer was no longer her problem. She had transferred the problem to me. It was now my problem.

I arranged a private meeting with Brenda's boss and confirmed what she had told me. He admitted meeting with her over the past few months but insisted she couldn't handle more responsibility. He was unable to describe even one of her ideas, which led me to believe he never tried to understand them. He was stubborn, and he was defensive. It was increasingly clear he would not change.

I wanted to move Brenda up, but felt I couldn't make her the old-timer's instant peer without hurting him deeply. I still respected him. I valued his years of service and the contribution he had made. So, appropriate or not, I did the next best thing—a lateral arabesque, a sideways move to save Brenda without doing too much damage to the old-timer's ego. I sliced off some of his responsibility and created a new job for Brenda. She would be responsible for all new store installations and report directly to me. Her boss would retain control of all ongoing educational activities. Eventually, when the old-timer retired, Brenda finally got the promotion for which she had been working.

If, in her presentation of the problem to me, she had shown any disrespect for the old-timer or disdain for his experience, tenure and what he had accomplished, I might have shut down completely and not been open to hear what she had to say. Had she come to me without having first tried to talk to her boss and work with him in spite of the limitations his style created, I would have sent her back to square one to make the effort. Had she come without proof of her ability to make a contribution, I would have sent her back to do her homework. Brenda Carol did everything right.

When You Have More Than One Boss

It didn't begin that way. Carol Vasquez had to learn to be schizophrenic. Carol, you see, reported to two bosses.

According to the company's organization chart, Carol reported directly to Roger Kennedy, and Roger reported to Kurt Schreiner. But, Kurt believed anyone who reported to one of his people also reported to him. As a consequence, he had no reservations about going directly to any of Roger's people when he needed something, and he went to Carol Vasquez frequently.

He'd stop at her desk and ask her to drop what she was doing to work on a report, or do some research, or follow through on a project. He didn't seem the least concerned with the impact it had on her regular work load, or even think of reviewing her other assignments for the purpose of setting priorities. As far as he was concerned, his things were the most important. This put Carol in an unpleasant bind. She was forced to put Roger's assignments on the back burner while she attended to the ones given by Kurt. Roger's desk was just 30 feet away and he could see Carol from the glass enclosure which constituted his office. When Kurt stopped at Carol's desk to give her work, she knew Roger was watching and she knew it made him angry, but she had no choice, no control. Carol was in a difficult situation. She had two bosses and she believed there was nothing she could do about it.

Unfortunately, this scenario is all too common. As president of my company, I also committed this sin of intrusion born of too many things to do and not enough time in which to do them. The appropriate question here, however, is what should Carol do in this situation?

First, she should *not* attempt to bring her boss and her boss's boss together to talk about the problem. Even if she uses the most respectful language to explain how she is sometimes put in the middle, she should not bring them together. Even if she uses the most rational explanation that, unless someone who is familiar with all of her assignments establishes priorities there is a risk that important deadlines will be missed, she should not bring them together. Bringing her bosses together to discuss what is obviously poor behavior on the part of one or both of them creates a confrontation in which she should not be a participant.

What Carol should do in this situation is really very simple. When a boss comes with an assignment that requires some work to be put aside or postponed, that boss should immediately be informed, respectfully of course, as to what the other work is and who assigned it, and the question should be asked, "Which of these assignments would you like me to do first?" This puts the responsibility for setting priorities exactly where it belongs—on the shoulder of the boss. If the junior executive is making the competing assignment, it requires him or her to relinquish first place to the senior executive or take the matter up with that executive. If the senior executive is making the competing assignment, it requires him or her to set the priorities or temporarily defer to the junior executive and discuss the matter with that executive later. In either case, the burden of resolving a potential conflict between bosses is left to the bosses.

*   *   *

Summary

When you have a bad boss . . .

1. Set your own agenda, schedule your own meetings but inform your boss of every move and involve him or her whenever possible.
2. Keep frustrations and negative thoughts to yourself.
3. Be assertive when necessary but remain as non-threatening as possible.
4. Increase your visibility to other executives and to your boss's boss. One way to do this is to write memos summarizing your progress on a project or providing information useful to others.
5. Don't ever go over your boss's head unless you've first talked to your boss and given him or her adequate time to respond to the problem, and you have decided there is no other alternative.
6. If you do talk to your boss's boss, be prepared to demonstrate how you can be of greater value to the company.
7. If you do talk to your boss's boss, never speak disrespectfully about your boss.
8. If you get competing assignments from two or more bosses, don't bring them together to resolve the conflict. When a competing assignment is given, let that boss know you have other work and ask him or her to set priorities or resolve the conflict with the other boss.

Chapter 16

The Truth about Opportunity

Great opportunities come to all, but many do not know that they
have met them. The only preparation to take advantage of them is
simple fidelity to what each day brings.

—A.E. Dunning

"You only get one shot in life, so when your chance comes, you
better grab it while the grabbing is good." That's the common wisdom—I use the term loosely—that has caused many an employee to
worry to the point of inaction about that one big break. It's a notion
which can paralyze anyone for whom advancement is important.

You've heard it said that, "Opportunity only knocks once." Balo-
ney! I don't believe it. I've never believed it. The truth is, opportunity
is knocking all the time. Each new opportunity may be slightly different from the last, yet we often get several chances at the same opportunity.

The real truth about opportunity is this: When opportunity knocks,
it always knocks *too soon*.

Think about it. Remember that job offer you didn't feel quite ready
to accept, or that speech invitation you didn't feel up to, or that house
you almost bought, or that business deal that seemed too much, too
soon? The truth about opportunity is it always knocks too soon. The
important thing is not to get stuck worrying about lost opportunities.
Opportunities will continue to appear and reappear, time and again.
Your task is to cultivate an open frame of mind so you are ready for
promotion opportunities when they appear.

Being ready to recognize opportunities so you can seize the moment is critical. Yet, when a job opens up in a company, too many employees do too much thinking and too little acting. The thinking goes something like this: "Aha! There's an opening in the department and it's tailor made for me. I've been here a long time, I work very hard and I've been doing my job very well. I, therefore, deserve this promotion. Management must be aware of the fact that I do a good job and are probably thinking about me for a promotion. It's probably in the bag. I'll just wait and see."

Convincing yourself that your promotion is "in the bag" is the first of many mistakes. The second one is waiting for something to happen rather than taking the bull by the horns and going directly to the boss to ask for the promotion. Another mistake is wasting a great deal of energy talking about the possibility of a promotion with your fellow workers, your husband or wife, your friends—all people who have no power to bring those thoughts to fruition.

Waiting around for good things to happen is like believing in Santa Claus. It's the worst possible result of having learned the BE GOOD— GET REWARD lesson. It's every employee's "Cinderella Complex," and it diminishes entirely the employee's real chances for success. Good things don't just happen. You have to make them happen.

Our company, which started from nothing and grew to national prominence within our industry, went through many kinds of changes. Our enterprise changed, and our people changed. As we grew, we were forced to accept new challenges and face new problems. There was no magic. Nothing came easily. Each major accomplishment was merely the sum of a thousand tiny accomplishments, most of which seemed insignificant at the time. We guessed and experimented and gambled. We had no crystal ball. We tried to avoid mistakes but, when we made them, we did our best to repair the damage and tried again. And, somehow, little by little, piece by piece, we grew.

Looking back, our company's growth was matched by the growth of our people. The maturing, the evolving was simultaneous and almost identical in the way it developed, almost identical in pattern. As time went on, I was more easy-going, more forgiving of myself and others when the things we planned were more difficult or took longer than we expected. In part, this was because I began to understand how growth occurs.

The Nature of Growth

It seems, before things change, before people change, there's a period of stress, strain and uncertainty. It's as though growth and change are always preceded by pressure which, when released, results in new attitudes, new confidence and an improved ability to handle bigger things.

Imagine blowing up a balloon. It's always easiest at first. And then, as the balloon nears full size, inflation becomes more and more difficult until the balloon reaches full capacity and feels as though it will burst. Now imagine that suddenly, through some miracle, the balloon changes into a bigger balloon. In a split second, the rubber has become more elastic and is instantly capable of expanding beyond its original capacity. The balloon, almost with a sigh of relief, expands to twice its original size. And, still, there is room for more air.

So, you blow again. It's easy at first but, gradually, as the balloon approaches capacity, blowing becomes more difficult. Suddenly, the rubber again becomes more elastic and, with a sigh of relief, the balloon expands to twice its size. And, still, there is room for more air.

And so it goes, the pattern of growth and change, always straining and difficult until, with a sudden relief, we are ready for more responsibility, capable of bigger things.

Unless you know you are not up to it, be willing to accept more work and more responsibility trusting you'll grow into it. Don't wait for things to be perfect. On that day when you are least expecting it and your boss says, "Say, John, or Judy, or Frank, or Joanne, do you think you're up to handling that new job of ours?" there shouldn't be a moment's hesitation. "Yes sir!" you should say. "You bet I am. Yes ma'am! Let's talk about it. I've got some ideas of my own," and, "I want to know more about what you expect," and so on.

In reality, you may be scared to death and think privately, "I don't know if I can really handle this new job. How am I going to learn all that I have to learn? Who's going to do all the work? I already feel overloaded." These kinds of feelings are normal. When people are promoted to new responsibilities, it's natural to question one's own abilities. But being ready for promotion opportunities requires a commitment to accepting the promotion when it comes. Unless you know you're not up to it, be ready to answer affirmatively when the question is asked. Just say "yes." As long as you know you can swim, jump in with both feet. It's O.K. Do the dog paddle if you must. You can learn the breast stroke and crawl later.

How Smart Employees Create Promotions

For the most part, promotions don't come as a complete surprise to employees who get promoted, the best promotions rarely do. Good promotions don't fall from heaven like manna, and the wise employee knows this.

Many promotions are actually created by smart employees. If you are working beyond the defined limits of your job description, looking for ways to do things better, accepting new responsibilities as they are offered and staying visible, you are working on creating your own promotion. The easiest promotion for the boss to grant is the one that merely actualizes, gives form and title to existing responsibilities. These promotions often follow a good deal of preliminary discussion and interchange about the problem at hand and how it should be handled. It is in this interchange, prior to the promotion itself, where the best promotions are made.

The employee who understands this will look for problems in the organization—not to criticize, but to use as springboards for advancement. This employee sees problems as opportunities to demonstrate the desire to assume more responsibility, to showcase talent, to manifest skill and problem solving ability, and to make a valuable contribution to the company's growth. In short, this employee sees problems as opportunities to demonstrate that he or she thinks like a boss.

Every organization has problems. What a wonderful and fertile field for all growth-oriented employees. They recognize that within their organizations there are hundreds of organizational problems—problems that can become launching pads for promotions and financial growth, problems waiting to be solved if only people will discover them. And, if you know the truth about opportunity, you will understand that the best discoveries are those made before problems become serious. The maxim, "If it works, don't fix it," can be improved upon: "Fix it before it breaks."

If you want to get promoted, my best advice is this: Know for a fact that problems within your organization can be wonderful opportunities for growth if only you will see them that way. Start looking for problems, not so you have something to complain about but so you can find ways to solve them.

* * *

Summary

1. It's not true that opportunity only knocks once. Opportunity is knocking all the time.
2. The truth about opportunity is that it usually knocks too soon. Knowing this truth will help you change your expectations and stop waiting for the time to be perfect before you accept new responsibilities.
3. Cultivate a readiness and willingness to seize opportunities when they arise.
4. You can create opportunities for promotion by looking for problems in your organization.
5. Use problem solving as a way to demonstrate your talents, skills, desire and ability to make real contributions to your company.

Chapter 17

Making It Happen

Every noble work is at first impossible.
—*Thomas Carlyle*

Most employees work hard, do a good job and want to get promoted but most do not understand what bosses really want from those they would promote. There are many tips in the preceding chapters to help you become more effective and, therefore, more valuable to your company and your boss. The key to appreciating them is this: Make yourself one of the few who knows what your boss wants.

Bosses want people who can think. They want employees with the ability to see beyond the immediate event and behave in ways that promote the company's long term interest. They want people who value time and know how to get things done. They want managers who can make decisions and follow through on a project as they would. And they want folks who can communicate effectively, both orally and in writing, and who know how to get to the heart of an issue. They value natural people, honest people and people who are just plain nice because bosses need executives who can be team builders. In short, bosses want help and they promote people who can help them and their companies reach their goals.

Harry Porter shifted his position in the chair across from my desk and smiled.

"Boy, I feel all charged up and ready to go," he said. "Now the question is, how do I get started?"

"I think the best place to start is when you come back to work on Monday morning."

"Right. Monday morning," he said enthusiastically. 'It feels like a whole new job."

"Slow down, Harry. Don't forget about your regular job. You can't neglect the normal things you're expected to do. But afterward, when your routine assignments are finished and your regular responsibilities are under control, then Harry, then you can begin to do the things that will help you get ahead."

Harry took a deep breath. "O.K., let's assume my regular job is under control and I'm ready to begin. What should I do first?"

"Look around the office," I said, "and try to discover some things we're not doing in this company that you think we ought to be doing. And find things we're doing that we shouldn't be doing. Start looking for our company's problems. We've got 'em Harry, I assure you. All companies have problems."

"You mean like finding things we're doing which are costing us too much money, or where we're not making enough money, things like that?"

"That's the idea, Harry. They can be big problems or little problems. They can be people problems or systems problems; any problem which keeps us form being the best we can is a problem worth finding. We need to find better ways to do things. That's how we can keep growing, Harry, and that's how our people can grow. I want you to get to the place where you just love problems because you realize they are nothing more than opportunities in disguise."

"So, when I've identified our problems . . ."

"Then start tackling those problems as if you owned the place," I said.

"The whole idea is this: If you want to make more money, you've got to be worth more to the company. That's the key in a nutshell. Smart employees make themselves so valuable in their organizations they never have to fight for salary increases. Their raises come without asking because their bosses can't afford to lose them."

Harry pushed against the arms of his chair and stood up. "I have to admit it," he said, "I'm feeling a little scared."

"That's O.K., Harry. Everybody get's scared when they're facing new opportunities. I do too. It's human nature."

Harry took a long, deep breath.

I went on. "One final thing, Harry, I want to make you a promise. If you will help us become a better company, I guarantee you're going to move forward."

"It feels as though I've got a lot to do."

"There is a lot to do but you're up to it," I said. "I know you are. Trust yourself. Believe in yourself. You've got all the ingredients. You've got a sincere desire to get ahead and you seem willing to make some changes. And most important, it would appear that you are ready to start thinking a little differently—like a boss. You can't know how important that is."

Harry had a twinkle in his eye that told me he knew. "It's like that story you told about the difference between two employees," he said. "They both started in this company at the same time, for the same pay—but one of them wound up a vice president."

"And the difference between them, Harry?"

He was smiling. "I really understand it now," he said. "One of them came to work for eight dollars an hour, and the other. . ." He paused to add emphasis. " . . . the other came to work for the company."

"You've got it," I told him. "That is exactly what bosses want."

Harry looked at me and grinned. "You know," he said, "before I came in here to talk to you, I was ready to quit and look for another job. Somehow, I thought there wasn't an opportunity for me here. I thought if there was, I'd have already been promoted. I thought promotions were given to people who put in enough time. That's what I thought. I guess I never really understood. It's pretty much up to me after all, isn't it? I can get promoted if my promotion makes my boss's job easier and benefits the company. It's as simple as that."

Suddenly, Harry looked at his watch and stood up. "Holy smokes, I didn't realize what time it was. I'd better be going. I've got a birthday party to go to. My kids will never forgive me if I'm late."

"That sounds like fun," I said, grabbing my coat and briefcase. "C'mon, I'll walk out with you. I should be going too."

We walked down the front steps together and headed for the parking lot. "See you tomorrow," Harry said.

I waved and started for my car. Nice guy, I thought to myself. He really wants to make it here. For his sake, I hope he does.

"Hell!" I said out loud, "For my sake, I hope he does."

* * *

Barry Eigen co-founded and served as president
and CEO of HealthCall Corporation, building it
into a viable nationwide health care products
supplier and franchisor. A native of Milwaukee,
Wisconsin, Eigen earned a bachelor's degree
from the University of Wisconsin and an
M.B.A. from the Graduate School of Business
Executive Program at the University of Chicago.